EMPATH

Three steps to achieve happiness: healing, awakening and empowerment with a life strategy for sensitive people.

By **A.S.Cloe**

Disclaimer

The information contained in " EMPATH " is meant to serve as a comprehensive collection of strategies that the author of this eBook has done research about. Summaries, strategies, tips and tricks are only recommendation by the author, and reading this eBook will not guarantee that one's results will exactly mirror the author's results. The author of the eBook has made all reasonable effort to provide current and accurate information for the readers of the eBook. The author and it's associates will not be held liable for any unintentional error or omissions that may be found. The material in the eBook may include information by third parties. Third party materials comprise of opinions expressed by their owners. As such, the author of the eBook does not assume responsibility or liability for any third party material or opinions. Whether because of the progression of the internet, or the unforeseen changes in company policy and editorial submission guidelines, what is stated as fact at the time of this writing may become autdated or inapplicable later.

Table of Contents

INTRODUCTION

You know that if you find yourself picking up the problems of other people, you are empathetic. You're sad when they're sad, when they're smiling, when they're in pain, you're glad. It can be very difficult to figure out the problems from them and make life very frustrating as empathy.

Empaths fluctuate their emotional impulses spontaneously in order to match those of others. You suit the energy with theirs when someone is sad, frustrated, hurt, or happy to feel how they feel. Very often, this is done in an attempt to relieve the suffering of that person; to bear their burden on them. Sometimes it stems from a conviction that you have to feel it appreciates a person's pain. Nevertheless, whatever the cause, a very important lesson all compassion should know is that in order to ease it, it is not necessary to feel or witness the suffering of another.

How can you resist matching those around you with the energies? Using the entrainment theory. Training is characterized as the tendency of two vibrating bodies locking into phase and vibrating in harmony; as well as the synchronization of two or more rhythmic cycles. This idea is universal and can be seen in most circumstances in everyday life. Two heart muscle cells, for example, can synchronize in time. Grandfather's clock pendulums lined against a wall will start swinging together. People who have lived together for over a month will also have their menstrual cycles. A guitar string tuned to a specific note can cause another guitar string to vibrate when it is plucked, tuned to the same note but kept a distance away.

We can also see the painful manifestations of this. Have you ever been around someone in a particularly good mood, and you also felt good? Or how about the reverse where someone was really sad or angry around you and you started feeling the same way. We tend to call it "infectious."

Okay, this same "infectious" power can be used to help prevent you from picking up the problems of everyone else. If you keep your energies higher than the people around you, you will find that you don't dip down to pick up sadness, anger, pain, frustration, etc. In reality, you will find that they will begin to suit your energy and feel better when you spend enough time around these individuals! So how are you going to keep your energies high? You can remain in a healthy, cheerful, happy mood by doing all you can when someone with lower energy is near. Think of someone you love, count your blessings, imagine holding a kitten or a puppy or a child, or just remember that the best thing you can do for that person is to keep your energies high rather than dropping them down to their level. Misery may love company, but having a room full of miserable people is not very helpful. Be the torch, the bright light in the storm, and help elevate the spirits of that individual. You're both going to feel much better and you're going to start learning that meeting a person at their pain level isn't the best way to help them through it.

CHAPTER ONE

What is Psychic Empath?

Do you ever feel overwhelmed at bars, films, parties or crowds of emotions? If you're around other men, does your mood ever change? Do you ever feel a sudden loss of power when someone is around? Do you ever feel those around you physical symptoms? You may be a spiritual empathy if you can answer yes to any of these questions.

A person who is particularly sensitive to energy and its related vibrations is a psychic empathy. All thoughts and feelings are generating vibrating energy, and we are all continuously releasing it into the community. We all have an effect on everyone, even in complete isolation. You have no doubt heard of the influence of the butterfly, where a butterfly shifting its delicate wings in Africa influences the energy elsewhere. The same applies to our emotions, sentences, desires, and acts. Anything produced in or by thought in solid space has an energetic charge that becomes accessible to everyone. The empathy implicitly decodes and assimilate the power of others as if it were innate.

While strong emotions are the most energetically loaded, they are most often picked up and assimilated by psychic empathy. This is not a concern if the personality is one that has a constant positive outlook and a happy and joyful mood constantly. Such a person will be happy about others who share the tenderness, and there is no harm done.

Nevertheless, compassion often becomes troublesome for someone who has experienced a lot of life-long suffering and hardship. Such a person tends to gather highly charged emotions or even physical symptoms from those around them. Like a magnet, they suck up other people's emotions that reflect their own; and they often feel overwhelmed.

Psychic compassion, though many would disagree, is a blessing, not a curse. Energy healers, medical intuitive people, and spiritual therapists also possess this ability and use it in their everyday work. Such individuals will sometimes release from themselves and others they represent the negative energies. At the very least, compassion provides a basis for the practitioner to guide the healing process of the patient.

Are You An Empath?

What does it say to you?

Empathic people are sensitive to feelings. People who have always been sensitive can find themselves even more sensitive now in these changing times. And people who weren't that sensitive may notice that they're becoming more like that.

Sensitivity is a question of our time, And for the following reasons, I fully agree. It affects all sorts of people, genders, cultures. It is particularly prevalent in people who attempt to have a positive impact on other people.

It is triggered by people who imitate our unconscious feelings and beliefs more often in situations.

Why are you supposed to care about that? Okay, first of all, if you're not aware of it, it can explain some of the things that happen in your life that you may not have noticed before, such as unexplained mood swings like weeping for no apparent reason or being very upset about something that might usually just be annoying, increased exhaustion, insomnia, body aches and tension, and disease... It could also be very content.

It can affect your ability to be successful from a company or job perspective, connect with others, contribute to the world and have the desire to make it a good living. It can affect your ability to have fun, take part in physical activity, your friendships, and your well-being from a personal point of view.

And it's just a start.

What are the symptoms of compassion for you? (Sensitive to emotion)

1. Those who are emotionally sensitive often and profoundly feel emotions.
2. They know about the emotions of the people around them.
3. Sensitive people are easily hurt or upset. An insult or unkind comment will have a profound impact on them.
4. In a similar vein, sensitive people will aspire to do so.
5. Sensitive people are easily hurt or upset.

Empathic Psychic Abilities

What is emotional empathy?

Sometimes known as "empathy" is an empathic psychic. Empaths have the ability to feel and understand other people's feelings, similar to how telepaths can feel others ' thoughts. Yes, empathy and telepathy are psychic powers closely related to each other.

Clear-sensitive psychics ("clear-sensitive" psychics) typically exhibit empathic psychic abilities. Empathic qualities are uncommon, but not unforeseen.

Characteristics of an Empath Empaths show these characteristics:

Extreme sensitivity to other people's feelings

An intense awareness of their environment

Good comprehension of the language of the body

Solid knowledge of human emotion

The ability to feel deeper than others

The Empathic Spectrum

Not all psychics have the same empathic strength. Many psychics only have rudimentary empathic abilities, while others have highly advanced empathic abilities. Most of the empaths collapse in the middle somewhere.

Psychics with the most basic empathic ability can sense what another does and can feel their feelings at times. Only some of what others experience can these psychics understand.

Psychics with the most advanced empathic skills can sense all the emotions of others. Such psychics often become so interested in the feelings of people when engaged in empathic training that they briefly lose sight of their own identity. These psychics can send emotional messages and project their own emotions onto others.

Empathic Healing

Most empathies choose to use their ability to heal others. Empaths normally put their hands on someone to know how they think. The empathy can therefore explicitly concentrate on what the patient needs.

To ease their stress, strong empathic psychics will express other people's feelings. Loss and sadness are two universal emotions that can be communicated and alleviate by strong empathy. A psychic can also express their own emotions to spread joy and happiness in order to reverse this process.

A Curse or a Gift?

Because empathies spend so much time worrying about other people's feelings, they can forget to worry about themselves. Empaths can suffer poor health due to self-neglect, emotional stress, and physical tiredness.

On the other hand, it is a rare and wonderful gift to cure and spread feelings of happiness!

Now you've heard about compassion and cognitive empathy.

What is that meaning?

If you feel you may have empathic psychic abilities, you need to improve your abilities in order to discover your true psychic power. Otherwise, nothing useful will ever be your empathic strength! What a mess!

A New Approach to Emotional Resiliency of Empath Yoga

Maybe the biggest challenge in today's world is to feel all of life— joy, ecstasy, and bliss, along with frustration, heartbreak, and pain, and still keep an open heart — to stay fully awake, conscious, and alive. Yet many of us will be shut down, protected, reactive, and defensive without this conscious purpose. Yoga is a powerful tool not only to help us relieve pressure in the body and relax the mind but also to soften and open the soul.

Then, we were all wounded, feeling frustration, heartbreak, and loss. We begin to let past hurts influence our future without the knowledge and awareness of how necessary it is to let this energy flow through us, rather than shutting it down around us. Physically it shows up as we fall on ourselves in an attempt to protect our hearts from potential injuries with a slouched stance and rounded shoulders.

Most of us have received messages from the earliest age that it is not okay to feel rage, disappointment, anxiety, fear, or any other emotion that is considered negative. For many, it resulted in phrases such as "stop crying or I'll give you a reason to cry" or "girls don't weep" or even "stop being so emotional." We've been told with these terms and others that anything other than happiness and joy is not real, and so starts the guilt and shame that affects so many of our lives.

Today, as adults, and after a decade of deep inside suppressing our thoughts, many of us are bursting with what has remained untouched. Yet it keeps calling us, stalking our every step and peppering at our heels, waiting for us to pause for long enough to encourage us to catch up with everything we've been running from.

This would clarify why one of my new yoga clients shared frustration about why she couldn't seem to relax in the evening until she lost a bottle of wine or more. She was so resistant to being in the moment, as most of us, and dangerous feeling what rose to the surface that instead she decided to numb out, and this became her daily routine and the only way she could enter a pseudo-relaxed, peaceful state. However, as indicated by the fact that there are 14 million alcoholics in America today, she is not alone in her quest.

This is not the only compulsive behavior, which is why over 64% of Americans are overweight or obese. Even with these coping mechanisms, insomnia affects over half of the U.S. population, with at least a few days a week as many as 58% of adults worrying about sleepless nights.

But perhaps the most alarming statistic of all is that in the last 10 years, antidepressant use has increased by 800 fold. The tendency to disown what comes up inside impacts us at younger and younger ages, and unfortunately the fastest growing demographic is pre-schoolers.

All this points to the fact that it is time we stopped running away from ourselves. True emotional resilience means giving ourselves enough credit to realize that we can do what we need to feel, sure that once we do it and come out on the other side of it, we'll be lighter, stronger and more relaxed than ever before, maybe since we were children.

Such a disconnection between our bodies and our minds has grown, many of us are lost in an eternal stream of chatter of mental that is so busy, we have become like heads walking without bodies. In the feelings, the story, the idea, we get so lost that we no longer have a connection with our bodies or even feel them. Yet it's a connection to what's going on within our bodies that binds us to our heart and keeps us grounded.

Most of us feel that if we spend time and energy focused on caring for our physical bodies and intellectual pursuits, we are safe enough. Nevertheless, very little attention is paid to our psychological well-being, which is the very energy which drives us and influences the quality of our lives. For many, long after taking care of their physical body's needs and stimulating their minds with intellectual pursuits, the last frontier is mental wellbeing.

But we're living in a beautiful time. As the world around us is rapidly changing, increasing numbers of people are shifting their attention inward. It's the only place left to go when the outside world appears wild.

And no self-discovery quest can go far without being willing to recognize what we think it is. Something as intangible as a feeling can be easily ignored in a world with so much internal noise and external stimulation fighting for our attention. But we can never really know ourselves without a desire to see, experience and appreciate the complex force that passes through our bodies.

Our emotions have a meaning for us at all times. And if we choose to ignore them, our body will begin to send stronger, more visible signals that will ultimately manifest as pain in the body if ignored long enough. Denying our feelings is like keeping a beach ball underwater; you can't hold it down forever and eventually push your way to the surface.

All too often we wait until we are on our knees, exhausted from attempting to unsuccessfully force our will on a situation before we are patient enough to pause, pay attention, and begin to open our minds to the possibility of a new path.

This is what inspired Empath Yoga's birth, an understanding of yoga immersion and a course of certification. Empath Yoga is the inevitable culmination of almost a decade of work and practice throughout the world with individuals and groups. Empath Yoga students learn to create and keep the room for themselves and others first. The solution is simple: providing clients with a safe place to get in touch with their reality, feeling what they need to feel so they can come out on the other side of it and encouraging and motivating them to make powerful choices in their lives.

The sense of being lightness that comes from letting go — the pressure that we unknowingly hang on to in our bodies, the oppressive old tapes that we replay in our minds, and the emotions that we stuffed deep inside — is unlike anything that can be expressed in words. This needs to be heard. This needs to be felt.

CHAPTER TWO

Empathic Civilization

Empathizing is civilizing, and civilizing is empathizing, Early humans were hunter-gatherers, following the history of civilization, whose sympathy spread to their own tribes. People applied their sympathy to their religious affiliations with the agricultural revolution and the growth of the philosophical consciousness of humanity.

Citizens embraced the idea of nationalism and kinship with their countrymen with industrialization and the concept of nation-states. the time is ripe for human beings to expand our compassion to the whole human species with today's universal access and communication.

We seem to have developed our sense of empathy from the Indian background to include our families and the baradari of our caste. If our polluted roads and undisciplined traffic are any indications, our sense of larger community is still underdeveloped.

While some of us are connecting as a country-like in times of natural disasters and particularly for a big cricket match, India's empathy is still quite underdeveloped. So what would it take for us as a nation to make the leap to a sense of empathy for the human race as a whole?

Gandhi was a leader in demonstrating how to live inclusively and feel connected to the whole world. Unfortunately, in his own lifetime, his vision of an open and inclusive India was not realized. Is this a better time now?

If empathy is our natural state, it is logical that in our minds we have built artificial barriers that prevent us from communicating and acting on our intent. One barrier is the notion of Adam Smith that our conduct is driven by individual self-interest-with the invisible hand taking care of the whole universe. The evidence clearly shows the reverse. Empathy is our driving trait, not self-interest.

Out of fear emerges another obstacle. We believe charity begins at home, and only after reaching a level of stability can we claim to be empathic. This is also false, as the poor always lend far more support than the middle class or the wealthy to each other.

The rich have a greater social consciousness. For example, it was Ahmednagar's prostitutes who came forward to donate the earnings of one day for the Gujarat earthquake, pressuring the wealthy local businessmen to follow suit.

Essentially, deciding how we live and communicate is up to each of us as individuals. We got a choice. With our parents, we can welcome the entire world, or we can choose to separate ourselves.

The Connected Age creates a growing mass of people who consciously choose empathy. As this hits a tipping point, a noticeable and discernible change may occur. Express your own thoughts and experiences on a world of empathy.

Many Empaths Block Their Abundance

Empaths are people who feel profoundly and are souls that are incredibly sensitive. They feel pain in the words left unspoken, and somebody's eyes could slice the unkind look like a blade.

On this planet, they have a hard time here, always feeling isolated and betrayed by the spirit because many times the world around them makes no sense. In truth, it usually runs counter to all their intuition.

The reality is that empathies are detectors of human deception, not much is gone beyond empathy... Yet they will probably struggle to listen to their instincts and fail to act on their observations because they sometimes unconsciously do not trust themselves.

Empaths say we are spiritual experienced human beings and we are human experienced spiritual beings. Films like: Angel, Sixth Sense, What Do We Call The Bleep? The faith is illuminated by the City of Angels and others.

A healthy diet, exercise, and sleep are just as necessary to protect the soul. The only aim of the soul is to establish spiritual/emotional growth. The sense of joy and well-being emanates from the soul to the psyche. If the mind is neglected and malnourished by the spirit and the body ends up suffering.

Spirituality is the most effective way to heal the spirit. Spirituality is the science of God-related creation and redemption of the God-made innermost being-the center of us-"Made in the image of God. "Love makes, kills everything else. Loving can not coexist concurrently with other premises; therefore, only loving is God. The fly in the ointment of verses of human existence in divine form-as God-is the "ego."

Ego is necessary to overcome the physical life vicissitudes. The ego, though, is what causes us trouble. The reality is: all life on earth serves the sole purpose of cultivating our faith to the degree that it is free from religious indifference, free from selfish or harmful patterns of behavior (ego), free to return to our eternal home in Christ. Real faith in Christ contributes to freedom.

Like all beings, compassion expressed for emotional and spiritual development, emotional and spiritual difficulties is inherent in human experience.

Once values, perceptions, emotions, and actions are accessed and discussed at the unconscious level, the 'cause' of any and all symptoms and behavior is crystal-clear— the behavior and symptoms you encounter are mental/emotional, physical, or spiritual trauma/distress.

A Deep Healing process is a straightforward, succinct and direct method of transforming the cognitive, emotional and physical symptoms that transcend traditional methods while maintaining a clinical emphasis. Deep Healing avoids prescription and OTC medications, extracting body parts, artificial hypnotic inductions, and mental interventions. The method is directly related to a person's perceptions and needs. The method is down-to-earth, too - the-point, realistic, courageous and with 30 + years of successful holistic health protocol experience and centuries I know Deep Healing is undeniably reliable.

Get all your needless emotional baggage transmuted to the unconscious level and experience higher love and happiness vibrations immediately.

Explore why emotional wounds and traumas... Even the smallest bad experiences you've ever forgotten... You're taking your happy future, living the one you're supposed to live. (You're not going to believe how much energy you offer to these invisible forces.)

Uncover the reason(s) why conventional trauma coping is not just terrible, but dangerous. Afraid of your past? Find ways to clear up painful memories without reliving it or telling anyone about it.

(This is the magical path to peace that your soul has longed for, for years.) (It's like one of those tiny levers opening giant doors.) It's possible to transmute your blocks to the activation of abundance.

You must learn to -receive-hold onto money-find protection in this world and in your body Receiving it is safe for you!

Empathetically Empathizing Our Enemies

The human race is finding that the repeating of history is not working with regards to killing our own species. Although only one-percent of all the humans who have live on the planet in recent recorded history of 2000 years have been killed in a war; we still see the tit for tat, reciprocal responses which seem to transcend the generations. The best way to achieve political will if in fact you are willing to wait, is to make them weak through gifts or making their lives too easy, thus taking away their need to fight for their rights. Once this is achieved, they enter a realm of mediocrity and lose all motivations to fight, innovate, press on or wage war against you. Once you have a populous at that point you can slowly turn up the heat and all the little froggies will remain in the pot without jumping out until it boils over. Sure, they will bitch and moan about it as the heat gets too hot, but not a one will rebel or fight you for your agenda.

How do we know this is fact? Well we see it in the United States and the middle class who duly allows mediocrity to overcome them. We see this in nations we have rebuilt after wars, they become weak, enjoy their lives and demand the status quo not willing to fight the gradual changes. Those nations who wish to serve their will must take a long-term approach and empathetically empathize their enemy and then slowly over generations turn up the steam and modify their thought processes convincing them that they are happy, free, lucky, better, smarter, stronger, enlightened. Once they have reached the purported created reality and perceive that they have arrived, they will no longer look towards fighting and you can then have your will with them. Once a nation or a culture reaches a point of instantaneous self-gratification for every humanly innate urge, they have arrived at a point that they are not willing to sacrifice that which they have for that which is right.

CHAPTER THREE

The Secret Weapon of Empathy

Empathy: A constructive approach as a method of listening through the process of being fully present for deep understanding.

The definition above is my own and stems from many years of practical and applied research. We used this concept of empathy professionally and personally and never sold more on a template of loyalty and dignity than that provided by empathy.

While empathy is nothing more than the ability to listen with our whole being to stand in the shoes of another and fully understand their reality, the art of this role is no small achievement.

As we've listened to people engaged in difficult topics of discussion throughout my adult life, we can usually tell in the first few minutes whether or not their conversation will be productive and successful.

In my experience of counseling and coaching couples, business partners, families, and executives, we are struck by how often the listener not only misunderstood what is being conveyed when debating a difficult topic but is also busy thinking about her / his response without being fully present as the listener. Generally, they are on the defensive and have to "prove their point" or "be wrong." The acute increase in frustration and/or anxiety is what results from this situation. Consequently, pulse levels begin to rise in the participant's bodies with noticeable pressure.

If the emotional environment is not controlled rapidly, the primitive brain engages (mammalian brain) and then individuals are unable to receive information from the expression (I'm going to share a lot about preserving the dialog's moral integrity in part 3 and 4 of this series). If there is no rapid recovery, the result will be a loss of focus on the subject and a deterioration in an emotionally charged fight that polarizes the participants.

In any conversation, emotional control is essential, and this can be accomplished by strong empathic listening skills. Themes are quickly lost in the heat of confrontation without controlling the emotional environment and nothing of significance is resolved. It is important to remember that the object of an interaction is to achieve a satisfactory outcome about which all (all) parties will feel good. Without this in mind, those who think they have "played" will have the absence of "buy-in." We saw more partnerships coming to an end, outstanding people leaving their jobs and families suffering because of the lack of buy-in from all stakeholders.

Empathy, by the essence of its purpose, is to help participants move through a system together. This serves to keep all stakeholders engaged in the conversation, keep them on the same page, and control levels of anger and anxiety. It, in effect, retains dialog credibility.

Empathy also allows the speaker to have a greater awareness and insight into their inner understanding of the subject under discussion. This internal awareness and insight are provided to the speaker when the empathizer expresses a genuine interest in what the expresser communicates in conjunction with the ability to want to know.

To be truly noticed and to feel understood is all too uncommon for most of us. We listen with compassion to our ears, minds, thoughts, intuition, and eyes. The perception includes the entire body and mind. We capture what is implicit or clear in this way, sometimes reading between the lines. It goes far beyond understanding the expresser's expressions.

As an empathizer, they are much less interested in listening to the words and much more interested in understanding the scope of the total experience of the speakers.

Listening without worrying about how we're going to respond, we can then immerse ourselves in the expresser's reality.

We've been working with a married couple recently who owned small businesses. For years they had been arguing around a recurring theme that had to do with recruiting contractors vs. doing all the research on their own. He was of the mentality that you work it out yourself when you take on a task. No matter how long it takes, no matter what price you pay (loss of sleep, loneliness, irritability, etc.), do not hire consultants to be paid by the client.

On the other hand, she worked from the viewpoint that obtaining assistance and support was an essential part of how she learned and gained new knowledge to execute the company's required strategies and plans. Since we had them working with empathy skills (along with other forthcoming skills in future newsletters), there was new understanding and knowledge inside 3 meetings that produced a good negotiation.

Even after 20 + years of marriage, this happened. She discovered that he saw assets as limited, including cash, and that his philosophy is that if you want to get something done, you're doing it yourself because his wiring was so overwhelming in fear of lack. He discovered that she often had fear and insecurity that she couldn't work out an issue by herself, and was also encouraged to always seek support and help in her previous career.

When they recognized each other's view of the deeper issues behind the dispute, they were able to negotiate how to tackle new projects. Until seeking consultancy, she agreed to try 2 or 3 different options and agreed to set up a budget line item for recruiting consultants in the company.

The depression of "not enough" had reduced once this was known and she was able to walk through her worries of not being able to figure out anything. Knowing that cash was available without a corresponding struggle, she was able to relax in trying new projects on her own.

When using compassion in a conversation, here are a set of tips to follow.

Give the speaker a genuine interest through eye contact.

Let the expression know your body language and be willing to understand (not to be confused with agreeing).

Attentively listen. Include those answers if you feel your mind trying to respond and remain in empathy. Next, you will be able to answer and then you will be given the same opportunity to feel understood.

Try to understand the significance of the location of the expression. This matters to him/her.

Listen to both the implicit and the specific.

Hear thoughts, dreams, aspirations, anxieties, and needs.

Formulate what it is like to be the person you listen to in your mind and body. It allows our self-centered role to be excluded.

After hearing what the speaker has to say, reflect on your understanding to ensure that you have correctly captured the reality of that person. Note, you're working together and knowing is the duty of your soul.

If the speaker corrects your misperception, just listen so that you can get the understanding that she/he needs you to have and then try to reflect it.

Becoming More Awareness of Empathy

Another compassion said the energies around him and the spiritual gifts he has become more aware of. Yet he was also afraid of it at the same time. To him, it comes from moral beliefs that convinced him they were not God's gifts-that they were from the devil. You may have been raised to believe that these kinds of sensitivities are wrong, but at the same time (even as a child) you have had a perception, emotions, and internal understanding. If so, you might be somewhat confused about how to handle their use. You may not have tried to develop these talents because you're afraid you're going too far or you don't know what kind of limits you're supposed to set.

Let's first take a look at Jesus, a beloved teacher. When a girl approached the hem of his jacket, once he was in a crowd of people. He knew instantly that virtue (healing energy) had gone out of him and asked, "Who touched me?" He felt it when somebody touched his electromagnetic field, even if she only touched his skin! The verse reminding us that every positive and perfect gift, spiritual gifts, comes from God tells you. There are many spiritual gifts mentioned in 1 Corinthians 13: the gift of prophecy, the gift of languages, the gift of language comprehension, spiritual discernment, healing, miracle work, etc. These are listed to our advantage as we know that in some way we have been blessed. And there's a responsibility of lovingly using those gifts. Such gifts were not offered to us to hide them from the world or to hate them. We are instruments for supporting us and others. When we have these spiritual gifts, it is very important to cultivate our spirit and set limits so that everyone out there is not bombarded with energy. Before we can love others, we must love ourselves, or else there is nothing to offer. It's like refueling a car to spend time with Goddess. Without more juice, you can't run very long!

Several people wanted to hammer him once Jesus walked the Earth, several wanted to crown him. There was a huge difference and what people thought of him. We empathies have the same dilemma. Others may not understand you. You might be afraid of the presents you've got. Through our religious teachings, we were taught that the discernment of spirits or the ability to communicate with those in the afterlife is of the devil. A close member of my family called me a necromancer. There is no gratitude for my gifts. Is this stopping me from using them? No, we use them because these gifts have been entrusted to us and we are responsible for using them wisely; and that is what we plan to do. Do we flaunt them before the members of my disapproving family? No, that's what the Bible calls the pearls standing in front of swine. I don't call anybody a donkey. I'm suggesting there's no need to bring something so precious out there and let your talents and sensitivities get stuck. You will determine to whom and to whom you use your gifts. We've made it a rule that we just don't do it unless we have permission to pray for someone. You can easily get your energy in somebody else's tangled by energetically messing with the things of another man.

Many people are highly energy-sensitive and see things or get hallucinations. They may know intuitively what happens in the life of another person. You don't have to support every person you meet, but you can do something. Pray about it before you plan to become involved. Breathe deeply for a couple of minutes and ask yourself if you have anything to do/say about what you've learned. How do you feel when you think you're thinking or doing something to help? Does that feel right? Do you have any pain or feelings in your body? If so, avoid engaging on a human level. You may not want your help if a person hasn't asked you to help them. Do you feel lighter, happier or better to support this person or to say what you have discerned? If so, ask for advice on what to do and how to treat the victim.

You may or may not need to address them on a human level when you keep thinking of someone and believe they need support. To lead their path, you can always give love and light. Only call the angels to help. Imagine a stunning beam of light, maybe pink or blue, coming from the universe. Pink is the heart of love; green is healing. See this light beam traveling to and around the needy person. This strong energy is like a stem cell with divine wisdom, knowing where it is needed and what to do when it comes to it. Not only does this give them the energy to work with, but it also gives them insight so that they can make good choices. They can feel the energy undergrounding and helping them. If something needs to change, however, they want to, they may apply the power. If it's healing, if it's a friendship, if it's emotional/mental, it doesn't matter, it's common in love and light. Give the energy and let them do what they want with it as they are guided by the spirit. You do not attempt to manipulate any outcome or alter anything in the circumstances of the life of another person by sending love and light. You don't abuse their free will or "fix" a situation created by their conscience to learn their lesson from. Sending someone positive energy is like leaving a present on their doorstep. It offers what they need, but they never know who sent the gift and you're not going to have to take on things from other people. You're going to know who and when to help and how. You can intuitively know how far you need to go with your help if you obey your internal guidance and what you need to do to reinforce your boundaries.

You must use your talents if someone asks you to pray for them. But instead of thinking or sensing with your body or emotional core (fourth chakra), use your sixth chakra, also called the third eye, to see or understand where you need to focus energy. We're going to be exhausted if we continue to work out of our feelings and our physical strength. But when we operate out of divine power, the sacred heart's location, it's not us doing the work; we're just a conduit. We can be the sun, and we are God by being the light. And we don't have to think about retaliation or worry about other people's thoughts.

So if you're worried about what your spiritual abilities have been taught or worried about what other people are saying, remember where God's laws are written. The rules about which the psalmist David spoke are not written on stone tablets or in a book, nor are they found in religion. They're in your heart published. If something doesn't feel right and you're in disagreement with it, go with the truth that your heart expresses to you.

The Missing Piece to Overeating - Why Diets Fail In Empathy

There's more to the face than approaches overeating and obesity. A big reason most diets fail is that mainstream weight loss programs don't make a difference in how we handle subtle energy, what Chinese medicine is called life force or chi. The body is penetrated and surrounded by subtle heat. In reaction to being overwhelmed by negative vibes, sensitive people that we call intuitive empaths unknowingly overeat. Empaths can not only feel the energy around them, but they also store it in their bodies. If this is you, when the temptation to over-eat strikes, you can be encouraged to concentrate and support yourself.

Here is the positive concept of obesity: they have less padding when empaths are overweight and are more vulnerable to absorbing negative vibes. For example, early twentieth-century faith healers were notorious for being grossly obese to avoid feeling the symptoms of their patient— a common trap that I also observed unintentionally falling into modern-day healers; food is a convenient grounding tool. Likewise, many of my patients pack pounds to defend against huge or minute distracting vibes. Power is at the heart of a desire for empathy. If your sensitivity too negative vibes are minimal or extreme, creating alternate coping strategies other than overeating is crucial for a diet to succeed. Here are eight tips from my new book that will help you cope with negative vibes without food violence. If assaulted by an angry colleague or a global threat, immediately apply them. Keep up with those who work best for you.

8 Halting Energetic Eating Emergency Interventions
If the urge to over-eat hits:

1. Identify an addictive craving from a True Need: a symptom of food neglect, addictive craving is a recurrent reaction to energetic overload. In the end, like a drug addict, you eat certain foods; this leads to obesity. Cravings sound intense: be wary if you start to search for candy and carbs in general. For example, chocolate, using it to self-medicate anxiety, or getting a sugar high—-also if you have mood-swings, sugar hangovers, you can't control your consumption, or you get sick. You eat to relieve stress with cravings, not to create strength. Start identifying and restricting addictive foods.

Such a storm and drang are lacking in a true nutritional need: there is no hunger or lung for food to defend against negative energies. A true need comes from a central location, has nothing to do with calming our feelings (comfort foods) or obsession. Feeling safe from food rarely requires mood swings—sedation or elation— rather a sense of satisfaction. A real need helps you to enjoy your meal, conserve energy, and not result in obesity.

2. Quickly identify intense stressors that trigger addictive cravings: ask yourself immediately: are you subjected to bad vibes? A stranger with a loudmouth. Experience of going through security at the airport. A blockade of your mother's overbearing telephone calls. Don't write off the "smaller" accidents that are famously sending motoring empaths to the fridge. Eviting panic. Identify the cause and effect of methodically. Negative energy doesn't have to victimize you. The trick is to clear it once you've been fooled as soon as possible.

3. Breathe out of your system negative vibes: take a five-minute break to control the damage. Inhal and

exhale slowly. Breath stimulates positive energy as you have learned; it also removes negative vibes. See if they're trapped in a particular part of your body. For starters, negative vibes go straight to my gut; a toxic stun gun makes us feel irradiated. Identify the weakness of your points. Practice this analogy then: just as your lungs consume oxygen and remove poisonous carbon dioxide, you can breathe in light and clarity, breathe out the pressure. Respire in vitality. Exhale terror. Also, visualize the negative vibes that exit in my lower back between the spaces between the vertebrae. You can also try that. A successful cleaning process is to suck out toxic vibes. You are responsible for the flow. Permeate every inch of you with well-being. Perform this exercise until the harmful residue is safe.

4. Pray to remove the addictive addiction: go into prayer mode if you're caught by a craving. Breathe slowly for a couple of quiet moments. Give your heart consciousness and seek self-compassion. The desire

may feel unmanageable, but that's all right. Tell your higher power to bring it out of you in this calm state. There was no need for emotional nudging. A simple heartfelt demand works like a charm when you surrender your ego-involvement. What you do is call on a cosmically dominant positive energy to supplant a destructive drive of the material world.

5. Take a bath or shower: To immerse yourself in water is a quick way to remove negative vibes. My pool is my sanctuary after a busy day: from bus fumes too long hours of air travel to personal unpleasantness, it washes away everything. Waterworks on you as you relax. It has alchemical properties that purify the physical body and field of energy.

6. Burn sage: Just because you can't see vibes doesn't mean you don't feed over them. Try burning sage to combat somebody deposits negative energy in your office or home— a tactic that has held pounds off my patients with lots of people-contact in their room.

Vibes accumulate and, if not eradicated, may cause stress. You may not know that the subtle energies left over cause unhealthy eating patterns, but these vibes prey on you subliminally. Sage was used cross-cultural by the ancients to purify sites. Burn it, and the creeping negative vibes ' desire to eat will wane.

7. Visualize a Defensive Shield Around You: Visualize white light from head to toe covering each inch so that negative energy is unable to penetrate this shield and deplete heat.

7. Eat with Accord: Build a diet that suits your nutritional needs. I would like energy to inspire you to feed, more important than taste or any food dogma—a priority to be given to children. Everything you put in your mouth, go through your energy meter; see what is either nourishing or depleting. Even foods that you have shunned become more enticing as their power lifts your awareness.

Food is not a comfortable place to be. You don't have to let toxic fuel hide in you. Make a daily check-in to stay on top of your meal. Stay alert with negative vibes for cravings. Check your answers. Promise, it'll change your eating habits.

CHAPTER FOUR

Your Mood Impacts

Numerous studies have shown that people around them appear to see everything in a much more positive light when leaders are in a happy mood. The resulting environment creates a positive workforce, which in effect encourages improved overall productivity, innovative thinking, and more effective decision-making. The argument is often accurate when the depressive moods of a leader prevail: they have detrimental effects on the leader, his or her employees, and the quality of the company.

In 2000, New York University's Caroline Bartel and Michigan University's Richard Saavedra researched 70 workgroups through various industries. Our research found that in two hours, people who assemble in regular meeting settings end up sharing our good or bad moods. The fact that people working together share their moods has been corroborated by other studies.

Leaders must recognize that moods that emerge at the top continue to spread rapidly throughout the workforce within most organizations. The explanation for this diffusion is that these moods are observed by almost everyone in the business and are therefore directly influenced by them. Leaders who are unaware of this cycle fail to understand their impact on organizational performance, as well as their moods.

A large body of research suggests that most leaders are unaware of the significant effect their emotional intelligence levels, moods, and attitudes have on workers and the company. Leaders may remain confused about how they have the potential to communicate across an enterprise.

The consequences of unattended or unregulated negative behaviors are severe in many cases. For fear of the emotional reaction and possible anger of the leader, workers may be reluctant to share reliable and practical data and information.

To the degree that the leader is emotionally disconnected from the company, the effects of negative emotional responses are damaging; as a result, he or she will not have a clear sense of what is happening in the workplace. Such situations are particularly disturbing when employees work deliberately to conceal mistakes, errors and potentially troubling patterns.

Lack of Awareness

While an emotionally detached leader may often think that something is wrong in the workplace, the exact cause remains elusive, thus weakening their effectiveness. The perceived situation instability often causes leaders to second-guess their workers. Other serious organizational challenges can be triggered by the following reasons: lack of awareness If leaders show a lack of personal awareness, they can not objectively gauge their moods let alone the effect these moods have on the organization. A lack of awareness in some cases is the product of the ignorance of the leader, but more often it is a consequence of older styles of leadership being used.

Most leaders who fall victim to a loss of awareness believe like their private moods are the responsibility of no one. Because these leaders do not see the need to pressure themselves to please their workers, the burden of coping with the moods becomes their employees. Whatever the cause and purpose, a lack of personal knowledge not only undermines the efficacy of the leader but also their organization's bottom-line results.

Lack of self-management

It can be detrimental to a company if members have a lack of self-management skills. Mood swings, highly emotional reactions, rages, and outbursts affect both workers significantly and negatively. Leaders allow their emotions to dominate them in all these instances. These uncontrolled feelings weaken the confidence and morale of the worker, which has immediate and negative effects on the performance of the company.

If leaders allow themselves to be emotionally unstable, because of increased stress levels, their company may experience higher rates of absenteeism and employee turnover. This measurable effect can be measured, quantified and illustrated directly on an entity.

Lack of Social Awareness

There is a lack of social awareness among leaders if they fail to empathize with workers and other people. Those who lack social knowledge are either unaware that there is an issue in this field or do not care about the impact that their words and actions have on workers and the company. Leaders who focus only on performance while neglecting personal contributions show this social deficit actively.

These rulers are incapable of inspiration, ethics, or personal issues. As a consequence, they are often surrounded by inexperienced and afraid workers. Rapidly abandon the competent individuals or those with better job opportunities. Serious and clear will be the effect on the competitiveness and profitability of the business.

Poor Relationship Management

Bad Relationship Management Leaders with poor relationship management skills are unable to effectively communicate, resulting in misunderstandings, uncertainty, and conflict. Employees may feel leadership less and uncommitted in this situation, as the leader frequently criticizes and second-guesses their job. The bad relationships between the leader and staff ultimately decrease morale and motivation. Employees don't know where these members are standing with. And this feeling also leads to the high turnover of workers and lower productivity.

Although possible, it is unusual for leaders to show symptoms in just one of the above areas: they are typically deficient in multiple categories of emotional intelligence. Their impacts are exacerbated when these influences are combined; thus a toxic organizational environment is created which is filled with problems and disputes.

Such leaders also cause extreme confusion and disruption within the company as a whole. This not only diminishes their prestige and productivity as a leader, but it can also completely undermine and ruin the efficacy of an organization. Turmoil and harm will continue until the dissonant is replaced by a more optimistic and rational ruler. And this change is usually the only viable alternative for alleviating chaos and repairing the organization.

How to End Pain and Be Happy

Most people who believe in karma (the principle of cause and effect if you believe in previous incarnations) have the idea that the bad things that happen to them are a form of karmic debt. Either in business or relationships, they deserve whatever bad things have befallen them. I thoroughly disagree with the notion that what happens to you in this lifetime is due to the past life debt you have to pay off.

That doesn't make sense because we don't know what we've done if that's real, and we won't have any feelings of regret or repentance. How to be happy and end the pains of life is often accompanied by this statement.

Happiness is in your mind, but first, we have to overcome our mind from its propensity to focus on negative thoughts to experience it. The only way to put an end to suffering is to see things as they are objective.

Purely intellectual, emotional pain. You feel pain when you don't get what you want. When you embrace what you get, though, you're not going to feel pain. It's just true. When I consider what I get without any hesitation, opposition or negative emotion to it, I can't feel any pain from it. So we can infer that pain is caused by ignoring or dismissing a situation's objective reality.

Taking all that comes into your life, every occurrence as it is, instead of saying, "No, I don't want this, I want it," and you're going to end all your life's suffering. It has nothing at all to do with karma, it's all right in your mindset here and now and all in your head.

The notion of karma and past life debts is merely reasons for resisting the surrender of impulses and acknowledging that you are simply going against the reality of the situation. People say, "It's my fault that she abandoned me," or anything that went wrong. "It's karma, and I'm paying a karmic debt so I should suffer because that's how I could apologize and escape the karmic debt." That's just a justification for one being able to suffer or feel self-pity without thinking that it's self-inflicted suffering that could be prevented just as easily. If there is no suffering, there is no other alternative but pleasure left by the natural law of opposites.

The truth is that the pain is felt because you don't just accept things as they are and you have to give up your selfish desires and accept your fate to end the pain. It's just a child who wants all to go their way and throws a temper tantrum if they don't get what they want. It's because so many people stay at a five-year-old maturity level that there's so much needless suffering in our lives.

Instead of improving themselves, most people will put everything on the theory of fate or destiny, or that God hates them, remain the same, and continue to suffer for their entire lives whenever they don't get what they want. So they never have to make an effort to mature and embrace an adult's obligations.

In your heart, belly, brain, mind, and emotions you feel pain. The pain is an interesting fact. You're the only one that knows that. Others may have some sympathy for you and sympathize with your suffering, but if you're happy, they won't have any pain for you. The suffering in your mind is everything.

Which means you're which pain's root and master. After all, nothing enters your mind except through your intelligence which interprets the situation and gives it a taste of good or bad after passing the test of satisfying or rejecting your desires.

"You're either with me or against me, friend or foe," as they say in the films. Friends make me feel good, enemies make me angry. What if you changed your motives to decide whether someone was an enemy or a friend?

Let's imagine you're driving down the road and you're being chased by someone. You're trying to get away because you're afraid they're going to attack you. You get more and angrier and hate the person every second as the chase continues. Fear and anger keep building until your pursuer finally gets up to your car's side and holds up your handbag. You immediately realize that this horrible person who wanted to kill you is just someone from the coffee shop where you lost your bag unknowingly and he's just trying to get it back to you. Your view of the situation will change your feelings entirely when you think it's an attack or a relative.

We can't always have what we want in life. That would mean that everyone on earth, as well as all governments and the global economy, has to go the "I" way we want it to go. I think at this point we just got down to about two years old.

If I'm brave enough... Grow up! Life won't go the way you want it, you won't be God or Planet Earth's supreme leader. Changing the way you think takes just a moment. Understand all that is, that you can't always have what you want, the psychological suffering is triggered by not getting what you want, even for the death of a loved one. So embrace everything as it is and live with it as it is. In this way, your life will be free from mental pain and suffering, and the law will be peace. Grant it an effort. You will find your life slowly and gradually shifting, little by little, day by day.

Are You an Animal Empath?

you might be an animal empathy.

1) Whether you swear you and your animals understand what the other thinks or feels,

2) You know what your animals are talking about.

3) You also notice strange animals, particularly when you see them in a magazine or on television.

4) You and your animal companion have started to look and/or act in the same way.

5) Sometimes, even if you have plenty of room to move about, you feel trapped.

6) Talking about bugs you find yourself.

7) Look into the eyes of an animal and feel that you see a spirit.

8) You like more animals than humans.

9) You are strongly associated with certain animal forms, e.g. butterflies, rabbits, cats, cheetahs, etc.

10) Animals like you, even if you never want another. (This involves "adopting" furry friends of other family members despite your gruff manner and lack of attention.)

11) You are suffering from insomnia and eating chicken.

12) After eating animal products (meat, fish, eggs, milk, bee products), you feel sad, angry or nervous.

While many books and research are investigating links between food and nutrition, I have found a recurring pattern in Clinical Intuitive clients: wonderful people on religious journeys suffering from "inexplicable" anxiety and depression. We went to psychologists, often sought prescription drugs, read books of self-help, avoided sugar, and tried to implement the law of attraction, but to no avail. Most adopt vegetarian diets, or "eat fish at worst," but there are still feelings. Regardless of how optimistic and relaxed, they seek to behave, they feel a nagging sense of shame, sadness, and fear underneath. The more the person is tuned, the worse the feelings are. This reality was counter-intuitive at first until further research became intuitive "hits." Such highly sensitive, caring clients and students had become animal empathy.

Their symptoms are greatly improved by changing their diets in specific ways.

The power of food is experienced by highly sensitive people. The more healthy your diet and lifestyle, the more energy you can have. Therefore, on a spiritual path, conscientious vegetarians often suffer worse than people who are less mindful of their meat. When a vegetarian has unexplained anxiety and/or depression, we generally have to ask if they know about conditions in dairy farms or egg factories, including organic ones. Will they know the fear and anxiety that are rooted in their cheese omelets and imitation pepperoni pizza, regardless of convenience? Will they know that even tracing can build up quantities of those feelings over time? Then tell those who eat fish, "Have you ever looked into the eyes of a fish or seen a fish wriggling on a hook? Does that feeling appear familiar to you?" Most of these people admit feeling shocked at the abuse of animals and wanting to go vegan but do not think they have adequate resources. We claim that with a vegetarian diet and free-range food we have reached a "happy medium." Unfortunately, they are still eluded by "happiness."

Anything short of a strict raw vegan diet is going to do for some men. Others can make up for their current diet with a few tweaks.

How can you say this spectrum where you're sitting? Experiment!

1) Remove and reintroduce animal products for two days. Pay attention to your immediate reaction and feeling the next two days. When unsure, ask others to watch your mood and attitude without asking them why you want to know. When neither you nor anyone else observe a change in your strength, attitude, degree of appreciation or satisfaction, or how animals react to you, then you can stop or continue to experiment— your selection.

2) When variations are evident (lighter, stronger, happier, less nervous, etc.), then you can start by blessing your food and thanking it. We praise the

animal's spirit if Native Americans or other indigenous tribes kill for meat. If you want to continue eating food, milk, and eggs, then kindly remembering the sacrifice will help you do that in peace. There are two approaches to tuning in to animals. If you can sense the animal's impact on the material, you can also adapt to the spirit of the animal to give you a brief thank you.

3) Take a look at your present symptoms and see which animal feed can contribute to that energy.

Commercial chickens, for instance, are very high strung animals. Individuals with insomnia and anxiety are often found to eat decent quantities of chicken. Yeah, other factors come into play, but often enough I have seen this trend to mention it here. Most people are less nervous after increasing their chicken intake. When you work in a cabinet and feel squeezed into corporate demands, it becomes even more satisfying to stop chicken.

Another example: consider avoiding turkey if you feel confused or sexually embarrassed without any real satisfaction. I'm just going to share that factory-farmed turkey reproduction requires some odd sexual interaction without going into graphic details!

You may want to stay away from dairy if you have difficulty accepting blessings. Many people take up the sorrow of mom cow that her milk is going somewhere besides her calf. Instead, by rejecting valid blessings and wealth coming their way, they blame themselves for "stealing."

When you denounce yourself personally as being a killer or someone who has committed a horrific, unpunished crime, stop eating all pork products (including bacon) and see what is going on. Pigs have three-year-old children's intelligence. While eating ham, sausage, bacon, ribs or pork chops, people whose psyches report their knowledge may experience very low self-esteem.

4) Eat raw fruits, berries, nuts, and seeds. You will eat fewer animal products naturally and all these enzymes will give you the strength and insight to cope

with other emotional factors. Whatever else you eat, you will enjoy fruit and green smoothies, new salads and raw cacao. Simply add these items to feel more plentiful than lacking.

Was food the root of all mental or emotional struggles? Of course not! I have found a wide range of unintended triggers, but even small shifts can have a huge impact on animal empathy.

CHAPTER FIVE

Empathy of guiding Teen Towards Career Happiness And Fulfillment

What will our kids be when they grow up? Is it still the same as for us to go to college and get a degree for many? Will all our kids be doctors and lawyers? One of the most important things to keep in mind is that with the impressive technological advances many of the jobs our kids won't even have yet to exist. But one thing we have to teach our teens to think out of the box is for sure.

We must first be able to identify our strengths and weakness to think out of the box as parents. As Goethe said, "From those we love, we learn best." Are we content with our professional pursuits? Live and teach love for the trade! A very stable job was left to make good money to start my divorce and parenting coach company. Was it frightening? The answer is a resounding yes, but my intent, if you like, is what I'm good at. We need to help find theirs for our children. How are we going to do this? Help them first recognize their strengths. Should you employ a math tutor if your child fails math but receives an A in English?

Psychologist Martin Seligman's research says no. Instead, he suggests having your child in a creative writing class. You encourage the unique strengths of your baby. Education research comes to the same findings which concentrate on the relative strengths of children rather than engaging in their shortcomings.

What are the strengths of your son? Seeing three kids opened my eyes to how different people are from birth. An advanced psychology degree was have, so we thought we were able to shape and mold our kids as parents. To some extent this is true, but all my kids are very different people with different strengths. Build a career college for your teen that can include ideas, images, words of things they like to do. Then look for a job that takes advantage of this. It's incredible the young woman who cuts my hair. She is twenty-one and the ability to cut and style hair is truly gifted.

Her father and mother have both advanced degrees. And in college, her daughter never did well and she never liked it. She makes sixty dollars an hour at twenty-one. She has hours of versatility and is using her inborn imagination. She's found her professional passion and she's both happy and successful. But it took her parents to also be flexible and embrace her aspirations instead of demanding that she pursue theirs.

What if when they grow up, your teen doesn't know what they want to be? Support the study and understand. Many online surveys help people define their types of personality and what occupations these characteristics lead to. The Myers Briggs Interest Scale is one of my favorites. Ask the young people about what they're doing. Visit and explore a local college career center. Let them encounter a variety of things to begin to understand their likes and dislikes. The Holland Code was developed by John Holland, a career counselor. This is used across the country by colleges and career counselors. Many people can broadly be grouped into six groups in his theory.

Realistic is the first. Some people like outdoors and work with expertise in engineering, sports, and manuals. It's the doers. The second is the forms of inquiry. We can work on their own and like to discuss thoughts and problems. In math science and analytical skills, they may have strengths. Investigative, rather than thought. Second, we have styles of music. Such people are artistic, unstructured and innovative, like my hairstylist. We tend to be directed by their emotions. Creating artistic like it. Then there's the type of society. we choose to be around others and support them positively and contribute to society's better. We appear to be good communicators and ten to be extremely empathic. Societies enjoy caring. Instead, we come to the businessmen. We excel in leadership, management and persuasion roles. We prefer to be competitive, comfortable in themselves and like to be decision-makers. Ultimately, the Holland Code says that there is a person's traditional style. We prefer events that are planned and coordinated. We like to have a clear understanding of expectations and follow procedures that have been developed. We may have good numerical and verbal skills. It's the planners.

They need to help our youth understand who they are and see their unique personalities to start expressing their dreams for a career. Most importantly, we must let go of what we feel they should do based on outdated perceptions and accept their professional interests so that they can not only excel but also seek their professional fulfillment.

The Relieve Emotional Fatigue of Empath Blues

"Decisional tiredness refers to the declining performance of the individual's decisions after a long decision-making session." This theory has been extensively studied in psychology where people, including judges for instance, who have to make a lot of decisions as part of their daily jobs, get stressed out over time and tend to make worse decisions later in the day. The mind gets tired and finds it difficult to assess trade-offs, a vital decision-making ability.

In a similar vein, the constant emotional information they have to handle may excessively trigger Empaths. This is particularly true for Impaired Empaths, who find it difficult to control the stream of feelings they receive from other people. Overtime may become inconsistent in their ability to respond appropriately to emotions, leaving them feeling powerless and depressed.

You could start feeling sad under an Empath blues spell without knowing why. You will also be more likely to feel down later in the day, waking up well in the morning but having a drop in your positive emotions as the day passes. Empath depression is usually temporary, but if left unattended, it can become chronic. Please note that anyone who feels depressed for a long time can suffer from clinical depression and should seek medical assistance as well as therapeutic therapy immediately.

So what can you do when you're in the Empath blues throes? There is a very common misconception that seeking to be "happier" is the cure for psychological exhaustion. In other words, you should try to think positively, even if you feel completely lousy. Have you ever been with someone trying to cheer you up while you were feeling sad? You kind of wants them to shut up and go, despite their best efforts.

This reaction makes complete sense when you consider emotional quietness, which is the absence of strong emotions, necessary to relieve emotional exhaustion. Feeling happy is a strong emotion and strong emotions, whether positive or negative, is what in the first place triggered emotional tiredness! Not only that, but it takes a lot of effort to try and cheer up on the spot if you feel sad. You're trying to jump to the opposite end (happiness) from one end of the emotional spectrum (sadness) while being drained, so you're more likely to fall flat on your mid-jump head.

Many Empaths are unfamiliar with the state of emotional stillness necessary to deal with emotional exhaustion. We are so used to being tugged in the emotional direction of all sorts that feeling nothing is always confused with feeling dead and blank. They wonder if there's something wrong. And yet, for the brain, this is no different from sleep! We need time to run out of body, mind, and emotions.

An empath is often, thankfully, very intuitive creatures. They're attracted to what's better for them. That's why if you're an Empath, in the four most powerful ways to relieve emotional exhaustion, you'll likely understand some of your impulses.

Being alone: Empaths want time on their own where they are less likely to react to other people's emotions around them. It doesn't mean you're anti-social and people don't like it! This simply means that you need to refuel before returning to the planet.

Make sure you have plenty of time alone to do something not stressful like knitting, gardening, baking, etc. I enjoy playing video games that need a strategy, but I don't have any emotional triggers. Be creative!

Being in nature: Most Empaths experience feelings of peace in nature, between trees and in large bodies of water such as the ocean or a lake. Good reasons for this! When it comes to emotional vibration, trees and water provide a perfect "white noise." It's like wearing a mask that cancels noise to block out people's emotions. I walk around my house 5 miles a week in the woods, rejuvenating and energizing me for the day.

Being physically active: by shifting your focus away from feelings and into your own physical body, physical activity can provide great protection against emotional exhaustion. The physical activity must be sufficiently demanding for our purposes to warrant your full attention. Rock climbing and yoga were my favorites emotionally relaxed practices.

Meditation: Meditation is a powerful way to direct the focus away from others. This can be very difficult for Empaths who prefer to check in with others at all times. At first, it may sound uncomfortable or difficult. But being able to create a quiet space inside yourself, whether by concentrating on your breath or following a guided audio meditation, will give you the space you need to relax your mind as well as your fragile emotional system.

CHAPTER SIX

How Do You Self Heal?

Self-healing is a great concept in both the holistic culture of healing and the positive world of healing. To be able to heal yourself, you don't need to be tuned to any sort of healing. It's helpful, and a good addition to your toolbox for your own ability to positively influence your life, but it's not needed.

It's about addressing the issues from a mind-body-spirit level of self-healing on a holistic basis of healing in your life. Let's begin with the principles of the brain. You work on a romantic relationship issue in your life, for example, and you need to focus on self-healing. For this to be truly understood and solved, you must first consider where the problems lie in the love issue along with your issues. You must first love yourself. You should embrace yourself, all things, even those that you don't feel are good or changeable, and accept everything about yourself.

For the body part, you can start by sending self-healing to your physical body as well as your love issue you want to address if you've been tuned to an energy form for healing. It's a system of two stages. If you were not attuned to any form of energy, this way you can still heal yourself. Sit in a quiet room, relax your body and mind, and start to breathe deeply. Reflect on and slow down your breathing. Place your hands on top of your thighs and focus on your body and breathe. This will relax your physical body's energetic fields and slow them down to begin their self-healing process.

You can work on things like meditating for yourself and the question of your love for the spiritual dimension. Start keeping a newspaper and write down all the things you want to concentrate on for yourself and your self-healing love problem. When you want to pray, instead of meditating, you can start through meditation.

Self-healing is about all aspects and in all respects concentrating on your body. It's not just one way that's right and the other that's wrong, but a total way to concentrate on yourself, your recovery, and the places that affect you today!

Easy Self-Healing Techniques

Every one of us on a personal growth path needs a toolbox of simple, effective and efficient strategies to help us get rid of and step beyond our problems and blockages. Several of my highlights are the ones below: YOGA POSITION FOR CALMNESS AND SLEEP •Lie on your back and lie over the right ankle with your left ankle.

- •With your right arm on top, your hands under your axes and thumbs on top, cross your arms.
- •Focus softly only on the body's physical sensations including tingles and twitches.
- •Make sure to use your favorite breathing relaxation technique.
- •Take the place for 10 minutes, put your fingertips after uncross the ankles in the position of prayer. Keep for a minute the place.
- •Notice that you feel calm and clear thinking.

THE POWER OF NOW Focus on your five senses.

- •What about you can you see? Look at the color, form, length, light, shadow, etc. specifics •Close your eyes and be mindful of all the sounds around you.

- •Notice physical sensations in the body–comfort or otherwise of clothes and shoes, temperature, chair/pillow pressure against the skin, etc.
- •What do you like?

During the current moment, when your focus is 100%, you don't care about the past or the future, and you can't feel anxious. Anxiety is an anxiety that has been moved forward.

The body maintains a biological memory of all the traumas it has experienced, both physical and emotional. There is no pain left in the body where the source of the injury has been addressed. And, when unresolved injury and pressure exists in the body, physical pain associated with the problem can be picked up. If we only learn to listen to their words, our bodies speak clearly to us. As well as the language of the links between the mind and the body, it can warn us anywhere in the body that it still holds on to a specific experience or is calling for our attention.

You can release and therefore overcome trapped emotions simply by quieting your mind, concentrating on an area of body pain and having the goal of breathing energy into that area. For added comfort and warmth, you may also like to put your hands over the affected area.

Exercise: Think about a question that has troubled you. Picture it vividly and get a sense of what part of your body has been hanging on to this issue's discomfort. Get a good idea of how this pain is feeling in your mind. Remember the level of discomfort on a 1-10 scale. Focus your out-breath on the area for at least 10 minutes or until you get a release. Re-note the remainder of the level of discomfort-ideally the pain will be completely gone.

PENDULATION

It works by making use of the trauma experience of the body and the resilience experience of the body to create a stable state. Cross back and forth between tightness, constriction and pain and relative expansion positions in the body to pendulate.

- First, discover and explore an environment of relative discomfort, then find a place far from, or feel the most different from, discomfort and tightness.
- Go back and forth and concentrate on each of the body's two positions.
- Add your breath afterward. Focus on the area of relative relaxation as you inhale; focus on the area of relative pressure as you breathe out (reverse the order if it works better) •Repeat this process at least 4 times, breathe in comfort or expansion, breathe out the tension.
- You may find that the initial pain has decreased dramatically or has gone away completely.

ASKING THE HEART Who WANTS

If I ask people where they think their soul is, most people will put their hand over their heart immediately. The heart seems to be the doorway to the spirit. Tell your heart what it needs when you have a decision to make, and this is likely to be a reflection of the answer of your soul. I have repeatedly used the following strategy and learned to trust the responses that I indirectly obtain in this way, even though the rational, analytical mind or ego is trying to tell me something else.

Relax in a quiet place were for at least 10 minutes you won't be disturbed and breathe deeply to relax and still your mind. Reflect on the heart as an observer and begin by posing a question that is an obvious yes or no answer, such as, "Is my name Daffy Duck?" The heart's feeling response can differ from person to individual, but usually, a "Yes" answer will induce a feeling of relaxation and expansiveness in the heart, while a "No" response will get a feeling of heaviness and/or contraction. To learn how your heart/soul interacts with you, ask some questions with clear yes or no answers. Then you're ready to ask something you like that needs a yes or no answer and you should be able to distinguish between the two.

PROGRESSIVE RELAXATION TECHNIQUE

This is particularly useful for people who find it hard to relax or just begin meditation. comfortably lying on your back takes your attention into your feet to your forehead and face muscles to the main parts of your body in turn. Clamp every area as hard as you can in series, then allow it to let go and relax.

A recommended sequence of stress and relaxation is foot arches, calf muscles, neck muscles, calves, buttocks, arms, lower back abdominals, face and forehead muscles.

MEDITATION

Meditation involves a detachment of the outer senses and a submission to an inner power. The meditative condition called an alpha-state, is a highly relaxed state of altered consciousness between waking and sleep.

There are many different types of meditation and playing with them all on various occasions is a good idea to retain discipline: -Repetition of mantra, such as "ohm" the sound of development or the keyword of an affirmation such as 'confidence.' Mantras help turn off cognitive intervention and are recommended particularly for practitioners of meditation.

Breathing exercises, mentioned above, concentrating the mind on the breath — Concentration on a fixed object, such as a candle flame— Quiet contemplation in Nature's place — Insight meditation engaging the higher self to solve problems and provide answers. Insight meditation is very effective for clarifying problems that have been complicated by the ego and conscious mind.

Focusing on a point in a river as seen from a bridge is a good introductory meditation. When debris bits (thinks) float along the river identify them and see them go under the bridge. Do not attempt during meditation to actively interrupt your thoughts. Through regular daily practice, the effects of meditation build up over time.

HANDING PROBLEMS TO THE ANGELS

For those people who believe in angels, it is very beneficial to gather all the energy of a problem you are dealing with in a ball and then actively hand it over to the angels to solve it for the highest good and give it back to you at a higher frequency when they do so. It allows problems to be addressed at a higher level and in much more creative ways that most of us feel are feasible. Fun to deal with the nagging problems of friendship!

How To Integrate Self-Healing Into Your Daily Life

During our daily lives, we all have our ups and downs, we enjoy the ups but not downs. What we deal with both is crucial, in either case, we can use each of those moments to help us grow. We can either be happy or over-excited if positive things happen and raise our egos. If negative things happen, either we can calm down and look at the bigger picture or get very angry and get lost in our drama. Our wisdom and experience in dealing with situations are the difference between choosing each direction. The knowledge brings insight, and when we have a basic understanding of the power of self-healing, the best experience will come.

It is important to understand how the law of attraction functions to understand the power of self-healing. We are responsible for creating our experiences whether we like it or not we draw good and bad things into our lives. This becomes better understood as we gain experience in applying self-healing but, to begin with, sciences such as quantum physics have shown how particles behave according to the observer.

Using the law of attraction as a guide, when we attract the right moments in our lives and then feel energized as a result, we can see when we do well for ourselves. So learning how to harness this power becomes the challenge. When we experience negative events, it only means that we have to focus on ourselves, and that's when we need to learn how to cure ourselves. Even a very well-balanced person is going to experience negative events, we all have problems to work on, that's why we're here!

If we can take responsibility for a negative event and see what we need to do, we can turn it around to gain momentum and positive energy from it. The first step is to surrender our defenses and ego when we feel pain from a case. Then we need to feel the pain and discuss it with our feelings, which in effect would add a great deal of energy to our consciousness where we can see it all on a better basis. Moving on with this, if we are prepared, we can let go of our fears. When we succeed, only partially, together with a sense of confidence and energy, we will feel a relief. We will no longer cause those kinds of negative things in our lives when we can cure ourselves fully.

We can see the strength we give to ourselves as we heal ourselves from our negative events and it will become addictive. All we need is to take the time to step back and focus on ourselves rather than respond to our egos, even if the reaction is internal. As we learn from ourselves, we gain a lot of insight and even empathy for others who may be facing the same problems that we have had. But up to that point, we may feel resentment towards others who respond like the ways we remember what we don't like about ourselves. That's a sign right there that from our dramas our core desires are to know and develop.

They also align ourselves with a higher purpose as they pursue our deepest desires to heal ourselves. That is when we can start to see how the attraction rule can help us take it to the next level. Self-healing increases our pulse of energy as we interact more with the world around us, adding more purposeful experiences to guide us. They are synchronicity phenomena, and when we remember them, it's very exciting because we think we're connected to a larger world.

Then the next challenge is to cope with the anticipation. The excitement comes in a type of powerful energy, most of the time it's going to be daunting that all we can do is give ourselves a satisfying boost to the ego. But the dilemma here is that anything that goes up has to come down. Letting ourselves into an ego boost shifts our focus when synchronicity activities are slowing down. The reason we eventually get into an ego boost is that we also have problems to work out for this purpose, where pride is the product of overpowering the insecurities that we may have. Once we can let go of our ego in some ways, then in the form of gratitude it is easier to let the energy stream into our entire bodies. Every part of the process needs that we be conscious of our egos where we need to be self-aware. It's a positive problem rather than a negative one. Then we use the same self-healing methods as when coping with negative issues.

It is therefore not only helpful but even necessary to incorporate self-healing into our daily lives if we want to grow free of our problems. We draw our issues, and to avoid the endless loops we need to fix what's inside. That sounds boring, but not when we start to see the benefits and steps towards a new reality. It's all about the conditions in which we are allowed to live and we have the power to change them.

This is a clear way of thinking that we can extend to every aspect of our lives, and when we do that, we will be more successful in everything we do. The one thing we all want more of is love if we can concentrate on it and develop it, it's going to be even better. It is both our source of power and our relation to a sacred universe. Love can't be found, it's a divine force that wants to come out in us, but it's constrained by our blockages that need to be fixed!

CHAPTER SEVEN

Psychic Awakening

Psychic awakening may sound like the experience of a moment that has long-lasting effects, but such an experience is typically the culmination of a lot of research that eventually' clicks' into place.

There's always the question of "waking up to what?" - integrated psychic awakening experience creates a new' person,' a higher level of awareness compared to which past life experiences appear as sleepwalking. How can a spiritual awakening be triggered? Boldly dream, plan completely, focus entirely, persistently work, rest deeply. It is all about equilibrium.

A' wake-up call' is similar to the waking experience; it happens when an external influence throws us off balance and causes us to see ourselves and the world with new eyes (although only briefly). Since the' wake-up call' experience of such a brief mental awakening is not backed by conscious work and progress, it does not last long before the' reset' to normality.

When you advance, you can see that you need to awaken to many different states and stages of consciousness. It's natural to oscillate between the desired state and the normal state before you incorporate and master a state. Such a back-and-forth, though, takes its toll. Don't be afraid of the swings of mood, just don't let them pull you off your course.

The desire for' psychic awakening' becomes a desire for' psychic dominance' after a while. There is no longer the duality of being awake or not, but as if several light beams converge in a pulsating mirror hall and refract to all sides, exposing wonderful forms.

Once you've decided that you will want to delve into your mind's energies, good news for you: you're psychic already! A gift from the human brain is the capacity to interpret knowledge beyond the five senses.

To achieve greater psychic sensitivity and accuracy, however, you must first figure out what is your greatest gift. You will be disappointed if you have the stereotyped impression of psychics seeing and knowing everything. That's not how it works.

Alternatively, in one region a psychic may have a powerful gift or in many areas relatively strong gifts. There are also a lot of different kinds of psychic abilities. We can interpret knowledge through our physical senses through our "mind's eye" (clairvoyant), our "mind's ear" (clairaudient) or even "phantom hallucinations" (e.g., clear-sighted or "clear smelling").

The above-mentioned abilities are not even all the kinds of psychic gifts that one might possess. If you want to become psychic, the first step is to research the variety of manifested psychic abilities and try to determine that one(s) is your best.

You have to practice using it once you have found your strong suit. For instance, if you're clairaudient, you'll need to learn how to meditate to clear your mind of its normal noise and open up and "hear" the sensory information that comes to you.

When possible, having an experienced coach or instructor by your side is always the best way to learn how to stretch your mental muscles. You can also buy different audio learning materials to help you in your search. Both techniques teach you how to protect your power from negative forces that may want to bind to you when they see that you are open to their broadcasts and are crucial to learning how to become psychic.

This is likely the psychic development's trickiest part. Once your brain is both a recipient and a message sender, it absorbs both data and energy without discriminating between "good versus evil" unless you consciously set up a filter.

So, moving slowly is the best advice on how to become psychic and unleash all your mind powers. Patience is required for this process. Find and start a mentor or some sort of practice! You're psychic already. You just need to assess and start building up your strengths. The trip is worth it and the reward becomes more spiritual than you could ever imagine!

AWAKENING PSYCHIC ABILITIES - WHAT THE BLEEP DO WE KNOW

Do you think you should improve your mental skills? We all have them to a lower or higher degree because the study of quantum physics proved that we are all related to the universe. In the movie "What the Bleep Do We Know," a fascinating point was made that the very thing (our minds) that perceives the material world around us is intangible in itself. The reason behind this lies in how the conscious mind of our thought functions. It's not the "brain meat" that allows the thought, but the hologram that the brain creates inside (and around) our skull.

Considering this idea helps us understand the likelihood of psychic abilities. The whole universe is made up of atoms and electrons that are informed by modern discoveries "pop in and out of existence." In other words, in time and space, the world is timeless- and our thought self's hologram is just another representation of this process. We are all related, therefore.

Other experiments have shown that the hologram of the brain is very effective. Scientists once stood outside a dying woman's room, hooked up to their brain activity monitoring devices. She prayed deeply as the end of her life drew near-but the most interesting thing was that her brain activity's performance registered a strength several times greater than your local radio tower's strongest emission. Therefore, in the world, we are all related.

They can be more mindful of this relation than the rest of us that distinguishes the psychic. The question then remains: Can the same knowledge be understood by "the rest of us?" Can anybody be psychic?

It could be equivalent to turning a TV or radio to activate psychic abilities. You need to turn both of these things into a specific band or frequency to get the software you need. The holographic brain of the human being is no different. Have you ever known that somebody is watching you or worried about you? Did you feel the phone is about to ring, or something odd is about to happen and does it? These are very small examples of the tuning of our brain to a particular universe frequency. It could be picking up the brain activity of someone else concentrating on themselves in the first instance. In the second, it's turning into a much broader energy output mix.

Psychics are people who either have a natural ability to become consciously aware of the many' signals' that are usually obtained at the subconscious level or have deliberately developed the ability necessary. Others cultivate this skill during puberty, while others have a sudden and quite terrifying wake-up in life later. It is suspected that this condition is associated with the pineal gland, also known as the "third eye."

The bottom line is, anyone who has an urge to awaken their psychic abilities will know it's within reach with the right kind of support.

Useful Psychic Abilities

It is very important at the beginning to understand why it is important to develop and use your psychic skills. We all have capabilities in the form of psychokinesis such as telepathy, clairvoyance, ESP and direct mind over matter control. Psychokinesis is a very important psychological capacity because it allows one to control matter directly with the brain.

We can see how important this is for all areas of life, especially when it comes to manifesting whatever we may need when we need it and whatever we deeply desire.

We all have hopes, dreams, and aspirations that we want to manifest and are typically hindered for some reason. Once we learn to use our psychic mind over matter powers, this blockage is easily removed. That's what this chapter is about. The best information I can provide about how your psychic powers can be successfully used and managed comes from his personal experience. Today, I've learned most of what I know about awakening and using spiritual skills in the form of yoga, chakras, meditation and working with the holy textbook known as "This Is PK." This book is one of the best ways to learn how to work with psychokinesis and mind in particular. Psychokinesis or "PK" refers explicitly to the energy of matter. This helps us to transfer objects at a distance, monitor and manifest through much easier, influence results, heal ourselves and others naturally and easily attract anything in your life that is necessary or deeply desired. I'm sure you can see how useful this unique psychic ability can be.

Then, we're all born with a lot of psychic abilities. These include the ability to project astral into other worlds particularly during sleep, the ability to manifest thoughts and intentions, natural healing forces. It also encompasses powers such as telepathy, psychokinesis, and clairvoyance. Several times, as a result of certain activities, these latent human abilities are stimulated, awakened and activated and even simply come into contact with pure knowledge or information. For example, some people have experienced intense psychological or mental phenomena over matter immediately after coming into contact with certain people, any data, or just doing certain practices like yoga, meditation, or chakra work.

The activation or awakening of our psychic abilities depends largely on our person and special Karma. Perhaps reading this chapter or following up with related information would awaken your psychic abilities and/or improve them. In any case, I can assure you that you will know it and you will not mistake it for anything else once you experience your real psychic PK energy. Such talents are very true to witness as well as very interesting. Including yoga, chakras, and meditation practice, there are many other methods for our psychic abilities to be automatically activated and ignited.

It is very important to know about these abilities as they offer us access to a whole new level of mental and spiritual energy. And this influence influences our life skills, resources, and good fortune rates. Many of these methods are addressed and are quite successful in the textbook This Is PK. The psychic abilities are becoming more than anything else a survival power. In this period, when we are all bombarded with so much material, deep intuition and inner wisdom are more important than ever. Such abilities can be of infinite value to our lives. Developing these higher abilities is, in essence, the first step towards living well in full abundance.

Also, through yoga and meditation and chakra training, his preferred method of dealing with his psychic abilities and improving them to the fullest. For several good reasons, I feel this way. First of all, yoga is one of our higher selves ' oldest and most effective methods of entry. The chakras are human nature's oldest and future mapping device. When I started to work with Lord Sri Krsna's mantra yoga and Bhakti yoga, his psychic abilities started to grow like never before. It was like a blooming lotus flower PK is very important to learn about because modern science takes it very seriously as a mental power that can manipulate matter and even affect outcomes by effecting the "chance" factor. PK is related to the quantum level of realization and learning how to rely on your PK powers is the key to real personal freedom and limitless prosperity. In reality, psychokinesis research has become a very important hot topic among people from around the world because it reveals the truth about what our minds ' energy can do. It has also become such a hot topic as many people, including myself, had personal experiences with PK and experienced it first hand. So of course, we're trying to find out more and know more and we're finding answers. Once you know your PK power is true, you'll learn how to use it and enjoy a life full of everything you've ever wanted and desired. In his view, reading from This Is PK manuscript and your personal experience is the best way to learn the truth about PK and how to work with your psychic abilities.

CHAPTER EIGHT

Awaken Your Intuition and Activate Your Psychic Powers

Developing your intuition is a positive way of taking responsibility for your life and using your internal psychic powers to direct your path towards greater happiness and fulfillment. Seven ways of awakening your intuition and triggering your psychic powers follow. Each is designed to help you get through your normal thinking brain patterns. To help you dig deeper into your instincts and discover your psychic powers, these approaches combine the thinking process.

1. Open yourself to Spirit and grow consciousness of your world of inner through prayer, meditation and a loving desire to live a life of service to all living beings and the earth. You're going to be shocked at the riches and happiness you're going to experience when you enter your inner world. Children are particularly skilled at discovering their inner worlds, so take your child— or your inner child — on an adventure of meditation wonders and deep prayer.

2. Using easy-to - do-crossover exercises to create the connections between the left and right brain hemispheres. Cross your right hand over your body's front and tap your left foot 7 or 8 times. Then cross the left hand over your body's front and tap seven or

eight times on the right foot. Perform the movements, but pass your arm over your body's back this time.

Use your non-dominated hand to do things, such as opening doors, brushing your hair or teeth, or even reading. You are also generating more brainpower for problem-solving and critical thinking skills in addition to opening more channels in your mind for intuition.

3. Each of your five senses ' sensitivity. Intuition may be called the sixth sense, but we can't expect the sixth sense to be sharp when our five senses are dull. Our lives give our five senses an infinite sandbox. Put the five senses together. Begin by holding any item, like a stone or piece of cloth. With that object, become intimate. Look at it until the eyes are closed to see it. Then ask yourself what you like about the artifact. Use your imagination. You don't need to place the substance in your mouth and taste it.

Mix it up once you've been through all five senses and ask yourself questions like: What color is your taste? Or what's the sound of the artifact like? Then go to the next step and ask yourself questions like: If this entity could talk, what kind of wisdom would it tell me about my life?

4. Be mindful of Spirit's messages by becoming more conscious of life at every moment. To help make your life better, be open to receiving knowledge and advice. Nature is a great intuitive educator. Take care of the animals that cross your path and the winged ones that attract your eye. When you stay in the midwest center and dip and dive a flock of seagulls around you, listen. Are you being told to let go of your fears and get up with them?

Nature is alive with people from rocks, trees, tree creatures, and a multitude of others who are still speaking to us. We just have to listen.

5. Record and communicate with the greater than you are: Christ, Goddess, a spirit guide, an angel, the highest self of someone you love and trust who has passed over. Choose to meet regularly. It's best to meditate after the night. Use your favorite blank newspaper and start writing, or draw if you're a visual learner. It doesn't matter what you're reading, writing, or drawing, and goes on for about three hours. Usually, it takes about three pages to resolve the obstacles in your mind that stop you from getting into your deeper existence.

You're going to feel the change and write a question once you're done, then write the answer. Just write down the words that come to you, don't judge the answer as you read. This is a delicate process. Don't look forward to yelling. Believe in what's coming. Go back later and read what you've learned. You will be shocked at the inner world's intelligence.

6. Play with yourself and other intuitive players. Ask yourself which line is the quickest before you get into line at the bank or market. Gather a group of photos of different people of the same gender, turn them upside down and guess which image is on the photograph's other side. To stay safe, use your intuition. We live in the land of deer. We slow down each time we hear the deer nearby. Of course, deer are going to be around the next corner or the next hill.

7. Let go of power and yield to the spirit-connected part of yourself. None of us control life, but we are responsible for our lives. We can choose to have the fullest experience of life. Or not. For what we have, we can choose to be grateful. Or not. We can choose to live a life of service to our lives and society as a whole. Or not.

Trying to keep hold is like trying to stop the flow of a river. Taking charge of your life becomes the master of your destiny, floating along the river and laughing all the way, and allowing your instincts to guide you to a more satisfying and fulfilled life.

It takes time and practice to take these steps to awaken your deeper instincts and activate your psychic powers. Be gentle with yourself and enjoy it. Tapping your instinct comes at your time.

The Best way to develop Your Psychic Abilities

The subconscious aspect of yourself has always been there, but you can not understand it unless you look "outside the door." The awareness of the world extends by reducing the fear of the unknown to gain knowledge of our other senses. That is when you can start to see the broader picture of your physical and spiritual life-a a higher evolution of reality. There's plenty of love and information waiting out there for you. A window of opportunity will open to a beautiful spiritual journey once the psychic senses are opened. All you need is the ability to be available, to learn, to free yourself from preconditioned thought habits, and to try and step "outside the box," as mentioned earlier. As with any project you choose to achieve, you need to combine analysis with training. The subject of learning psychic intuitive reading ability is a massive amount of material. Take advantage of every opportunity to broaden your mental growth skills with every chance you receive. Expose yourself to psychics and, if possible, get yourself a psychic reading. Research meditation and other methods of spiritual awakening. There are several seminars related to programs of metaphysical/spiritual research that can help educate you in the fields you are interested in. To help broaden your awareness, find a subject that best fits your needs and get exposed as much as possible. The more exposure you receive, the more by watching and learning from others you will improve your intuitive skills. The following list of exercises will help you develop your higher senses.

You're going to start sharpening your skills with a little training.

1) Start by tuning into your physical senses. Find a quiet place where you can be free to focus on a variety of scenarios. Stimulating the senses is the target. This will help develop your higher confidence in the project. Start with a few deep slow breaths, close your eyes, relax and imagine a wildflowers-covered open field. Imagine that you can taste the blossoms ' delicious fragrance. Listen to the breeze's gentle noises as it passes across the tall grass. Imagine the fresh air gliding over you softly. Is it hot? Maybe a chill is flowing through your skin. Hear in the distance the peaceful sounds of songbird as you lose yourself in the surroundings. Manifest your scenes by using your imagination and creativity. It becomes simple with training. Make sure you pay attention to the details of your climate. The exercise will help you to use your natural senses without being connected to the body. When exploring a range of aromas, concentrate on your sense of smell. Be imaginative and have fun with it while tapping into your imagination! Picture the sweet essence of an apple pie as it bakes, the clean smell of the wind, grass, petrol, a newspaper, freshly cooked bacon, brewed coffee, a pine tree, and leaves from the autumn. Experiment with a range of hearty spices. The aromatherapists rely on this exercise's benefits. Improve your touch feeling. Imagine holding a bunch of petals from the flower. Note the satiny, smooth texture in your hands, which is almost weightless. Then switch to an ice cube. Experience the abrupt change in the cube's cold temperature. Alternate this exercise between the two separate emotions. It depends on physical experience and touches several objects.

This exercise will improve your psychometry skills Try to hold someone else's worn piece of jewelry. Relax while holding it in your pocket. Do you sense the owner's energy? You might even pick up on their interactions. This became my method of first learning in one session of psychic reading. (This exercise makes your consciousness physical perception better than most other exercises.) It's easy to adjust to your sense of listening to music. Blues project, rock n' roll, bluegrass, cajun, Latin, jazz, and so on. Experience the music's rhythm and take the sound into yourself, almost as if it flows through your soul literally. Experience a ballad of sensual jazz. Hear the lyrics, hear the rhythm and appreciate the choice of the artist to mix the musical ingredients. Enable a classic masterpiece to calm your body in a complete state of contact. Try to differentiate the piece's array of articulated musical parts. Finally, when you do this exercise, you can aggravate the sensation of listening to "feeling." Your natural sight sense contains countless development opportunities. Watch the dazzling reflections on air, see the light as it bounces between the trees ' leaves, note shadows. Usually, you miss the little "stuff" with different eyes. Incorporate in your life the importance of light. One tree has plenty of green colors, not just one. Research the face of one loved one. Look at the fine details. Consider less interesting posts to see. Look out overflowing garbage can lying on the side of the road or a broken bottle. Enable your brain to take everything in. Reflect on the stars of the night as you watch the sun. Imagine seeing the stars above. This is so perfect for your spiritual tuning. Your sense of taste is important as well. Picture a sour lemon flavor, good coffee, bittersweet chocolate, buttermilk, a beautifully aged beer, sweet fruits, spicy foods, etc. Try a variety of foods and concentrate on your taste sensation.

2) Meditation practice. The practice of daily meditation takes a short time and can help relieve pressure on your brain, body, and soul. It's a great way to keep the energy flow of your body regulated and, if done properly, you're going to be revitalized and relaxed.

3) Remember your spiritual views. If you need to use your faith option for defense, please feel free to pray. Before beginning this path of spiritual awareness, it is hard for some to drop the emphasis on religion. Most were preconditioned to "not go there" by religious doctrine. There is a way in both to seek the balance. If you choose, and when you choose, you decide how to proceed with faith.

4) Believe in yourself. Understand that in this world we are all connected as one. You build walls that block your consciousness by staying separate, thereby restricting your ability to see beyond your thoughts. Spiritually open yourself and open windows to a wider spectrum of the reality of your life. Through gaining a receptive sensitivity in the physical experience, you will get closer to the ability to develop your psychic abilities.

5) Remember individuals. Watching people is a free entertainment card, so it should be a simple one. Find the perfect mall or park bench and just watch the people walk by. We are such different forms of the body, eyes, clothing, etc. Check them out... How are they communicating with each other? What does the body language on the "inside" tell you about them... etc? Isn't it wonderful how special that person is? Select someone you're interested in, someone other than the crowd. They may be sitting nearby. Research them without being over-evident. Try to read your word. This is a useful practice in outside reading people...

6) Observe wildlife. Go out and enjoy the wildlife. See a bird's flock. See how they communicate with each other and see how aggressive some are and passive others are. It is the law of nature. Among other research species. Chipmunks, squirrels, and bees. Make yourself aware of how all nature is linked to humans from the smallest ants, etc. The relation with all living things will help you to grow insight on this spiritual path. Practice reading other people after you have established your spiritual awakening. Sit quietly with your friends and try it. You can pick up bits and pieces from their situation in life. Ultimately, you must find out which aspects of your instincts are more prevalent. Maybe you're going to hear music they like or have been exposed to lately, maybe you're going to smell a particular atmosphere they're close to in everyday life, taste something they've consumed recently, or you're going to pick up on their emotions or circumstances from those around them. You're not so familiar with this test when you're comfortable bringing in others. You might just be shocked how far you have come in improving your intuitive senses.

Learning to Activate Your Inner Eye

Most of my followers, subscribers, and private customers will always tell me about learning to become a psychic.

It's one of my favorite topics... And to teach one of my favorite subjects as well!

Of course... You're going to read some people who disagree with my methods-and think psychic abilities should be shrouded in secrecy and the clear techniques of manifestation that I openly share... The general public should not be discussed at all.

The fact is, I think it's completely crazy. We are all born with the same soul of the same size... So our life experiences karma decides how well our natural and everlasting spiritual capacity is expressed and explored.

I want to show you one of the EASIEST ways to learn how to "read minds" and to develop incredible intuitive abilities effectively, easily and ethically. In the most caring and compassionate way, you can use this approach to begin seeing and experiencing the emotions, feelings, and experiences of others, and it is extremely easy to learn.

It's a simple idea.

Empathy is the REAL secret to psychic creation. The more empathy you have with others, the more you build an intense and emotional connection. The more you are related to someone, the easier it is to share energy and information with them in such a way that language and basic contact signals are passed through.

Empathy is about maintaining an emotional relationship with others that is about empathy, warmth, care, and compassion.

In reality, it's... Sometimes for this very purpose, you can hear psychics, mediums and clear-sighted people of all sorts CALLED "empaths."

Feeling empathetic is being compassionate and kind and being genuinely concerned with others ' well-being and health. THIS is the key to all sorts of epic spiritual awakenings, and all you have to do is be able to empathize profoundly with other people's suffering to trigger this spiritual gene.

Here's a very simple exercise I love for reading the mind directly. (Ethical mind reading-I'm thinking about sensing, feeling and communicating with the true spiritual self in another, and having an emotional exchange where knowledge is easy to see) The exercise is derived from the practice of RAJA yoga, a method of meditation that is often believed to lead directly to psychic powers. What makes RAJA yoga special is that it is often taught and practiced for the exact reasons above as an OPEN EYE meditation.

The yogis of Raja tell us that...

We live our REAL lives with our eyes open, and with our eyes open, we interact with others in the world, why should we learn to meditate with our eyes closed... If that's NOT how we in the physical world exist?

Here's how I do this:

1-Choose a mantra. It can be anything important to you spiritually. I'm quietly saying four simple words in my head as I do this exercise. To order to be effective, you can choose any mantra that is important to you it does not have to be a specific saying or scripture.

2-Keep your eyes open while silently repeating the mantra (although it can be if you prefer).

3–When you silently repeat the mantra with your eyes open, start looking at the sacred space between your eyebrows. Add to the small spot between your eyebrows the full force of your attention. Imagine the room opening up at all times like a glorious portal into the unseen world around us.

See the light in the room. (Note: this is the sacred place that most religions and wisdom traditions teach us in the spiritual center of the true self-where the divine enters and where there are enlightenment and awakening)

4-Continue to see light in this room. Focus... But don't be stressed or stressed... Only imagine the light that flows into that spot and fill your mind with a dry, inviting bright, beautiful and happy light.

5–Continue to focus. Keep repeating the mantra.

6 –20 minutes is the perfect time for beginners to practice this. I encourage you to do this first thing in

the morning, or before school, or wherever you go out into the world.

7–First, you're going to try to communicate with someone you already know psychologically and energetically. (It's always good to start with someone you know, like or have a comfortable kind of relationship with, as you most likely have an established karmic relationship with that person or a certain level of trust and relationship that will make the process a little easier)

8 — Focus on the place between your eyebrows when you see them. See if you can give them "shine" quietly when trying to connect with love and care.

9 –That sounds stupid... But if you can, and it doesn't look strange, smile with someone you know and like while doing this exercise.

10–Look into the sun now.

Can you see that?

Do you hear it like that?

Try to project your light into their sacred space (the point between the eyebrows) while also trying to become a source for the energy that they unconsciously emanate.

When you begin to do this well, and it will happen REALLY... You're going to know that. Most people begin to see an aura-or even a bright angular light like a halo around the people with whom you have a very energetic band. (Others record many interesting and innovative spiritually transformative encounters far beyond the reach of this short instruction:-) RAJA Yogis and meditators will inform you that this emotional relationship is the real dance of the divine... And the easiest way to enter a space of shared mind where knowledge, intuition, and awareness are a clear flow of insight and enlightenment.

CHAPTER NINE

The Intuitive, Psychic of Children

Are you kids with "special" skills? If you're new to the concept of sensitive kids or indigo children, you might need to know the difference between emotional, mental, and mediumship.

Most kids now come to the world with an intense sense of awareness. Not just physical stuff, but spiritual things. By that, I mean, through their spiritual eyes the children see. Through their spiritual senses, they feel; through spiritual eyes, they also hear.

I understand it doesn't always make sense for some of you. But when you know that humans are not just physical beings but have consciousness and spirit, you can also recognize that on those other dimensions there are beliefs. There is also knowledge of mind and spirit.

Have you ever looked at a conference speaker or a presentation? Normally you only see the person: the speaker's physical body. You see the clothes he's wearing, the way he's holding his head, the motions and gestures he's wearing while speaking. This is natural. We don't dream of it. We became so used to seeing only with physical eyes, we refused to see any other way.

But sometimes, if you're focused on what he's saying and have a strong sense of connection with what his message is, you're looking at him. The attention shifts to the text, so the key receptor in your brain. Your eyes are shifting into a separate, lighter consciousness. You're open to who's thinking about the fullness. All around him a halo starts to shine. If there is a solid curtain or color drape behind it, it is easier to see. This is the aura, of course. It was always there. But you can only be sure of this now.

Another example: did you ever go to a large people's room? You see all of them. But you also think something is wrong. You don't know what it is, but it just doesn't feel right. You find out there was some kind of trouble when you decide to leave. Your knowledge of this sensation has kept you out of trouble.

The kids see, hear and experience all kinds of things most of the time. It's not just because you had it once in a while. We are continuously tuned to the higher frequency.

So what does being intuitive mean? Psychic? Mediumistic, particularly as it relates to children? It is possible to combine all these talents into a general category: being psychic. While psychic means a specific thing, it is used to define all the abilities of metaphysics. Let me share some things to look for in keeping with these different skills.

Intuitive: It is being intuitive to learn something without outside awareness of it. Being intuitive is a subtle way to unintentionally touch energy fields to learn knowledge and understand things around you. It's so subtle we normally explain it away. We all have that power. But all the time our kids are fully connected to this capacity.

Their boys, connected with higher intelligence, often stream through their experiences. We don't have to organize their thoughts, we just obtain them. Sometimes associating what is happening with the child becomes hard if you don't know what instinct is in your own life.

Psychic: The next stage in creation beyond instinct is psychic ability. It is an understanding of innate knowledge and a willingness to work further with it. You have to remember that you are using it. Third-dimensional waves are embedded in the plane of the earth and are easily accessible by spiritual means. If implemented, it can be reinforced over time.

Psychics have access to magnetic energy from the fields of human and non-human energy, also known as the aura. By sensing or seeing energy patterns in the environment, they interact, knowing anything that happens in the life of the person. There are past life energies as well as future possibilities being introduced by purpose and aim set in the higher realms.

When demonstrated with intuition, all people have a degree of psychic ability. Others know it, and some don't.

Do you ever go to answer the phone and wonder who's calling (if you're not looking at your caller ID)? Do your dreams come true, sometimes even?

Have you ever felt like someone at the grocery store is staring at you, and when you turn around, a person looks at you down the aisle? These are psychic ability examples. It's just understanding or thinking something without getting any other awareness of it or being able to explain objectively why you know it.

The medium deals with a person's or place's energy vibrations. It interacts with slower waves of earthly frequencies. Psychics are in contact with living people's earthly vibrations, especially those of close friends or relatives. This also involves becoming mindful of spiritual forces that have been imprisoned and reside in the astral realm that is nearest to us as third-dimensional beings.

The children may see and identify lower entities that have failed to advance into the spirit realm in their development. When we think we can see them, some of these people like to interact with us. A child should understand that he can refuse to engage with that entity and ask it to leave.

A baby will also learn fascinating knowledge about events in the world and you, being intuitive. He doesn't understand how intrusive your vibration can be. This is when the child needs to learn about personal boundaries, not just for himself, but for others ' integrity.

Mediumship: A medium deals with spirit power or a lighter frequency than the earth plane as opposed to being psychic and interacts with spirit, typically loved ones who have died, spirit guides or higher beings. Psychics are not always media, but psychic media can be psychic as well.

Mediumship is aware of and accepts messages from the waves of spirit beings. It's a dead loved one's contact through an intermediary. Then the information is given to those who complain about the loss.

The main purpose is to provide acknowledgment after the physical death of continuing life and to send love and encouragement.

The connection with dreams, creativity, and spiritual awakening is rendered by constructing this bridge. It helps you to improve your spiritual path. It helps you to be responsible for honesty in your contact dealings.

Association with the higher realms also provides a firm basis for communicating with finer vibratory beings and spirit instructors. Lower-level energies will not be drawn to you as your relation with higher vibrations has been created.

Certain explanations for open communication with living spirit beings are to provide evidence-only facts that those still in the body accept. They produce externally perceived external behaviors by humans.

Such events are often regarded as paranormal activity. They manifest to be defined in physical form. Just because the child sees and interacts with spirits, this does not mean that the child is a medium. It only means that he has press habits. Such skills need to be developed, learned and mentored, properly understood and used.

Most young children who know spirits are continually seeing them and can be confused by it. On the other hand, most professional mediums enter the spirit world at purpose at specific times. When required, the child can learn to open up and shut down their abilities.

There are many variations between parents who don't understand what's happening and their kids who don't know how to describe it. The better it is for all concerned, the more you can read and study and challenge your children. Please love your kids and let them know that you're there for them.

Develop Psychic Abilities Via Meditation

The road to learning how to cultivate psychic abilities can be a long one, but to accelerate the process, there are several things you can do. This chapter explores what may be the best way to accelerate the cycle, relaxation.

There are a lot of different learning programs on how to meditate. We can be divided into two forms, passive and active, for the most part. You (or someone who directs you) control the flow of thoughts and ideas through constructive meditation by gently directing your mind down the path you want to take.

On the other hand, passive negotiation is a freer form and is probably the hardest to do for most people.

Human minds have been programmed to think, they like to maintain control, and it's much easier for most people to just stop and listen rather than seek to be an active participant.

However, when you stop and think about it, you must be able to receive information to improve psychic abilities. The details can come through thought, sound, sight, or feeling, but if you don't focus on anything else, you're better at all these things. By taking the time to keep the brain from concentrating on all the things happening around us and focusing on the minute forces flowing through and around us, we will begin to develop psychic abilities quicker than they develop on their own.

Many people rarely note the multitude of sounds nearly constantly going on around us. Our minds are too busy thinking about what to eat for dinner and getting ready for a big date and we're never paying attention to the fact that you can feel the air, even if it's just a tiny breeze or you can see the wind when you think your life is streaming.

You can hear the pulse of the world, the very rhythm of the universe as it passes through and around you, when you stop and listen, allowing your mind to become still. It sounds like a single note played on an angelic harp for me and allowed to vibrate to the ends of time. Some of my past students said it sounds like a message from the gods, carrying a single note throughout the universe. Others in the background sense a strong rhythm. A drum-like noise that makes them want to dance.

If you stop your mind from jumping from one thought to the next and encourage your heart, body, and soul to reach out and wrap your arms around the universe's life force, what do you hear?

Only find a comfortable spot to be in for a while to test it out. I prefer a quiet spot, but if you live in a big noisy city, just find the quietest place you can find and spend some time searching and making your body feel among the sounds of the city around you.

Whether you choose to sit, stand or lie down, it doesn't matter as long as you're comfortable. Yes, most people enjoy a calming walk while allowing their senses to open up to the world. I can't tell you how to channel the life force step by step, because how you feel it's special to you. Some will sense it, others will feel it on their bodies, and others will see it on a hot summer day streaming through the air like dandelion fluff.

Allow yourself in whatever way seems right to you to communicate with it. If you feel driven to concentrate more on a single context, do so. You can hear a sound, for example, and you don't know what it is. Enable the senses to trace the sound back to its source instead of shrugging it off and forgetting about it. The ears may not hear sound, but your intuitive senses may feel it and trace it down a stream like a ribbon of light. Was it a bird that you never saw before? Was it a tree's two branches gently rubbing in the air together? You will discover some wonderful things right in your neighborhood as your senses awaken.

To allow these things to happen, spend some time. Enjoy the experience and develop a desire to learn more, see more, feel more, hear more, and see your psychic abilities begin to grow stronger. Sometimes the road to developing psychic abilities is long, but if you take the time to enjoy the experience, it will give you a sense of peace and satisfaction like you've never experienced before, and if you're lucky your psychic talents will grow during the phase.

Empowerment Through Change

What does empowerment mean? Is it the same as the power of the individual? Or is it just an attitude that you take as part of some form of the personal development process from time to time? How can there be an appreciation for empowerment? Is there a means of measuring it? In reality, trying to define it seems a little tricky.

Okay, we know that through assessment, progress is being made and confirmed. Unless it can be proven, something cannot be accepted as truth. Just enough.

If something is difficult to measure, how can it be understood that there has indeed been any improvement? It may be important to avoid thinking about empowerment as a "buzz" word that gets bandied around to suggest some form of personal power to improve your skills.

The word' empowerment' has the word ' power.' Therefore, seeking empowerment means a person must have the capacity, willingness and desire to change something positive to gain more power. So if it happens, you can't become motivated if you can't change. Therefore, for me, motivation is about exercising your free will and making one or more positive life changes. It's not about taking other people's power. Personally, when considering the sense of equality, I think this often marks the basic difference between men and women.

I think it's reasonable to assume the relationship is now known between the mind and the body. Mind and body are different mechanisms, they work independently, and they can be viewed as two separate entities, but they form one integrated structure. Your mind is influencing your body and your mind is manipulating your body. That's all right, but how do we know this is true?

It can be confirmed that the brain affects the body directly. The common use of placebos is a simple example of this. Think you're being healed and the brain is responding and giving the body the good news. Recovery is continuing. Today, in this healthy, inspiring two-way relationship, the body still plays a leading, pivotal role. The body produces cortisol, the stress hormone, the moment you feel stressed. It is possible to measure and prove this answer. It is necessary to control the production of cortisol to avoid future medical problems. If you have an excess supply of cortisol in your body, you will be stressed in thought, feeling and behaving.

If you also add your thoughts, attitudes, and behavior to the mix of mind and body, you will get a clear picture of what is happening to the body neurologically, psychologically and physiologically.

This mixture generates your actions that derive your performance. So, it generates the results when you think, feel and act. And it's a personal choice.

Feeling motivated and exercising personal power is probably easier for men than for women. That is attributed in all sorts of areas to the bias against women. Nevertheless, women's empowerment is typically the same thing-understanding limits, deciding to be self-sufficient, and taking control.

Of reality, we also realize the persistent and unavoidable shift. When we know that we are free to learn any number of processes to build the change we need, it gives us a chance to become motivated. We can change almost anything we want, and at any moment, if we make the decision and take the change techniques seriously. It is the motivation to make these positive choices and to take action through them. Free will can work wonders and be in a driven state.

Acceptance of areas of our lives that need to improve and taking action to address these areas contributes to empowerment directly. Maybe it boils down to how we regulate how our thoughts and feelings are interpreted because these acts profoundly influence how we choose to behave.

Empowerment means accepting that you are in control of your life. Your feelings, beliefs, and values are the engines that decide how you think, feel, and act.

We need to encourage people to take full responsibility for the choices they make if you want to empower people. It can be deeply satisfying to inspire people in this way. We have free choice, and to know the joys of freedom we need to practice this.

A simple step you may take is to take some sort of inventory of your customs. Write down your good, undesirable habits. And take your good behavior credit. Well done! Well done! Now choose one of the undesirable patterns and either kill it or replace it.

This will result in prosperity in due course. How is this possible?.

Thoughts on Empowerment

People are empowered to make decisions affecting their job with minimal interference and second-guessing by others if given authority and responsibility.

It's overused and under empowerment? practiced word. We put their minds to work if individuals are motivated. They are committed to making decisions that affect their business part. They are taking responsibility for their actions. They work away from the tiny administrative burdens that reduce interest and waste time. In following the values of quality and service, they add value to the company. We are looking for ways to make a difference.

All companies need knowledge workers— men and women whose main resource is their ability to think and act on what they know. To solve problems and respond to opportunities, computer programmers, process analysts, accountants, attorneys, sales teams, managers, even workers in factory must use their best judgment.

Nordstrom's customer service is legendary because it allows and expects employees to make decisions that will make customers happy. To illustrate this point, a nearby Nordstrom store gives new employees a one-page employee handbook. This reads: at all times use your best judgment.

How Empowerment Works In Caught in the Middle (Productivity, 1992), I suggest that most people want some simple job-related things: purpose, performance, challenge and opportunity to learn, appreciation and acknowledgment, autonomy over their part of the work, association, and feeling they are part of a larger group.

Those six elements form the basis of all good efforts for empowerment. Remove any of them and weaken the dedication of the person to their job. Thankfully, what's good for the individual is also good for the company in terms of motivation.

Making Empowerment Work Build on the six basic things people need (these are mentioned above) Use these elements as a basis for all empowerment-enhancing initiatives. Remember, however, the following: simple sight and direction. The leadership of companies should understand why they want empowerment.

What do you want to do with it?

Which feels like strength here?

How committed are you to the realization of empowerment?

Is empowerment necessary, or would it simply be nice to have something?

Examine the activities of the company.

Policies. What is recompensed is finished. What is punished is stopped. Corporate policies and procedures such as assessments of results and changes in quality show people what matters for senior management. For example, when person is told to work together but their performance reviews place them in forced evaluation rankings against each other, will people protect themselves? interests. If you're pushing cross? Functional teamwork, however performance reviews only consider departmental work, the interdepartmental collaboration will suffer.

Unwritten rules of procedure. Those expectations tell people how the game is being played. People learn about the value of these unwritten rules as any written policy. A director will, for example, order workers to tell him or her the truth at all times, then continue to discipline the messenger who brings the bad news.

Structure. To borrow a phrase from the book of David Hanna, "Organizations are well designed to achieve the outcomes they receive." NUMMI is a highly successful automotive manufacturing plant based on high employee dedication and ability. This replaced a horrible GM plant where absenteeism stood at 25 percent the year it closed and where performance was a joke. Interestingly, it employed many of the same seemingly unmotivated employees from the old plant when NUMMI opened. The only major difference was how it was handled between NUMMI and its predecessor. To fix quality issues, people were free to avoid the assembly line. They are encouraged to learn a lot of different activities to add value to the assembly process. They've been motivated in short.

Why is it so hard to attain?

Once Tom Peters said, "We're just in the advanced stage of lip service." I agree. They are often afraid to trust others to do the job without scrutiny. I never met anyone who said he or she was improved by a comprehensive performance evaluation process. Yet most administrators assume that being used to inspire others is an essential tool. (If only those people were as trustworthy as we were.) Watchful eyes gave rise to dependency. As person tries to please dad and mom they fail to take the requisite risks and effort to help a competitive company succeed. People are waiting to learn what to do. As the sign in the office of a French civil servant read, "Never do anything for the first time." If five others are going to check, fold, spindle, and mutilate your work before it is accepted, why do you bother to do your best?

Our view of organizations is based on the chain of command and hierarchy. Those above you make the decisions, they are carried out by people below. This template is firmly anchored. I believe it's written in our DNA sometimes. Only when we see that it operates against initiative and motivation can it change, and when we can step back and take a cold sober look at how our actions can build the addiction and mediocre results that we despise.

There's Hope There's a business revolution going on. Since the seminal book of Peters and Waterman, In Search of Quality and our discovery of W. In the early 1980s, Edwards Deming experimented with ways to increase the participation of workers. Even with empowerment ideals, the federal government is trying to reinvent itself. Many organizations thrive, some struggle, but from all of them, we can learn. Such courageous companies and organizations have living lessons that can point the way for new organizational models that treat people with dignity and respect— and represent business interests.

Here are some examples of how others use motivation ideals.

Big adjustments in the process. Organizations like Corning are having everybody (or at least a representative sample of all organization levels) in a room to reengineer their portion of the business. Since this planning process includes those who need to implement the changes, opposition decreases, and dedication increases, planning and implementation time is shortened, and the reliability of the project often far exceeds what might have been generated by outside consultants or a small team.

Inter-functional teams. Organizations like Conrail are putting talented people from the center of the company together and inspiring them to solve pressing market challenges. These groups are more than task forces— they are capable of proposing and enforcing reform.

Data exposure. Several companies are researching how work is done to streamline customer service. We develop new procedures to ensure quick access to the tools and information needed by the people closest to the job.

CHAPTER TEN

Empowerment Changes Your Life Forever

Perhaps you ask, "What are personal empowerment?" In term, empowerment is liberating yourself from constraints and living a life of suffering and taking full responsibility for everything in your existence. It's about not making excuses for things in your life that don't go right and doing something to change them! It's about choices; the choices you make about all facets of your life daily. It's about being in control of what you're allowing in your life; who you're associating with, what you're reading, what you watch on TV and movies, who your friends are, what music you listen to, what you're eating, etc. Why is empowerment so critical for these choices? You ARE your options literally.

A general definition: empowerment is a mechanism that helps individuals take control of their own lives.

Empowerment is therefore about realizing that there are options in which you have the right to be the healthiest and happiest person you can be in now. The past is the past, and it can't be changed, so the emphasis is on what you can do right now. Which decisions you are now able to make to motivate yourself. You will gain greater control over your life when you practice your decisions and take responsibility and action. It had a million lies in her life for all the crummy. It blamed other people for her addictions to cigarettes, drugs, and alcohol. It blamed everyone for everything because that helped me to justify that it was okay in her mind. it was killing myself slowly to avoid confronting her problems, the exact problems it generated through the choices it made. It's a vicious cycle, but it can change through empowerment!

Let's look at a list of motivational keywords:

Self-Mastery

Personal Development

Positive Thought

Mind Power

Self-improvement

Spiritual Growth

Enlightenment

Responsibility

Law of Attraction

Self-Acceptance

Self-Esteem

Self-Discovery

Self-Strength

Self-Love

Self-Control

Own Choice

Freedom

Decision Making

Being Independent

Awakening

Ability Choice.

it is feeling out of myself. That's where it went wrong and it was going wrong for millions of others too. Through triggering this power inside ourselves, we have the strength and courage to make choices and act on issues that we consider to be significant. These issues can apply to every area of our life-relationship, economic, social, spiritual and physical. It is very important to understand that empowerment is a multi-dimensional process that involves all aspects of our being: psychological, emotional, physical and spiritual, and it is necessary to balance each of these fields.

A person engaging in life coaching, studying energy healing and mind exercises, attending self-help groups and workshops, home study courses, reading books, etc. can promote and encourage the motivation process from external sources. These courses must educate you and allow you to do these things for yourself upon completion of the course. You seek independence not co-dependence within the system because empowerment is a mechanism that evolves as we move through it. Dabbling in motivation is impossible to expect life-changing outcomes. For the full liberation of all pain and suffering, it must become a road, destination, lifestyle or way of life.

I've got a real-life story about "rags to riches." it learned how to conquer poverty, addiction, and violence to create the life it once felt was impossible for me. it is beat the odds because it is dared to believe and listen to MYSELF ONLY, which is the force inside! Do you think what it has done since it discovered the truth of self-mastery and empowerment? its am now a successful businessman, a published author, a global life coach, a specialist in energy healing and empowerment. "High school dropout, sexually and physically assaulted, druggy, drugs, welfare case" wasn't too bad for a once? That's the strength! It's about making choices that improve the quality of life.

Through independence comes understanding, and they do not mean knowledge of facts by experience, but the ability to perceive and appreciate facts, and to judge soundly and behave correctly in all life-related matters. Wisdom is the capacity to interpret reality and the ability to use the experience of facts in the best possible way.

Through wisdom comes poise, and the strength of right thinking, managing and directing your emotions, and preventing the difficulties that come from wrong thinking. Through wisdom, you can choose the right courses for your specific needs and guide yourself in all ways to ensure the best results.

The ripple effect is the magic of empowerment. By personal empowerment, you can inspire those around you to empower yourself as well by leading by example! Not only do you manage to change yourself, but you also help change the lives of your parents, family, and friends. You have the power within your community to break the chain of deprivation, addiction, violence, and misery. You will show them that where you were once helpless, by taking full responsibility and action over your dominance, you can gain total control over your life improving your situation. This will tell them that because you did it, it can be done! You lead by example, and your kids just know and repeat what you tell them. Consider them empowered.

Empowerment, The Structured Discipline

Just as an ongoing process is an institutional change, so is empowerment. To work effectively and efficiently, specific factors combine to establish a motivated atmosphere that must be in place.

Leaders should recognize that in contributing or withdrawing efforts, workers have a wide range of flexibility. Empowerment aims to inspire workers to devote as much effort as possible to the success of the activities of their unit and, ultimately, the company.

Within the context of their job description and duties, most workers would contribute as little as possible.

Through inspiring their workers, leaders are empowered to contribute not only to increased efforts to perform their responsibilities but also to more innovations, theories, and perspectives. It translates into sustainable success and improved results for the organization when collective strategies, innovations, principles, and experiences are integrated with an inspiring environment.

Leaders are the main impetus within their company to create an inspiring environment. We know that when such an environment is built at all levels of the company, the depth of empowerment is reached and that they have the power and authority to remove barriers to empowering their workers. The company will gain momentum in this way to step forward and evolve as a whole. The variables discussed below aid when putting in place to create an inspiring environment.

Employees Understand What Is Expected of Them

Employees must be encouraged to understand that a transition to an empowered environment is a key change for the company. Minimal efforts and sacrifices are no longer accepted — not as a punitive strategy, but as workers recognize their role in the success of the company and how individual efforts contribute to that success. Such changes are often accepted with cynicism, which changes when workers see that clear behavior reflects the words of the chief.

Employees need to recognize that deciding to engage themselves more actively by sharing their thoughts, theories and observations not only benefits themselves but also their colleagues and coworkers.

Goals and Measurements Are Consistently Applied

A critical factor of the motivated community is the clear implementation of targets, criteria, and measurements. This creates an atmosphere of confidence and integrity throughout the business when this is introduced as workers know that they are all treated fairly and consistently. We know what they are supposed to do and how they can assess those efforts. You know the consequences if you fail to meet those expectations. We are also conscious that they will be praised and honored if they meet the criteria.

Once workers know their organization and unit priorities, their team or workgroup's current performance objectives and goals, and the constraints on their decision-making authority, they are empowered to make clear decisions without input from the manager.

Employees Are Given the Skills and Tools to Perform Effectively

Employees Provided the skills and tools to work efficiently more than just a term, empowerment is a means of tapping in an organization's human resources. Employees can not operate in this setting without first being trained according to the principles of autonomy and teamwork; to perform efficiently, they must be provided with the skills and tools. Leaders recognize that it is a process that requires time to implement a fully developed, empowered culture. Training, training, tracking and improving the skills and tools that promote organizational change takes time.

Frequent and Immediate Recognition of Contributions

Recognition of achievements Frequent and Immediate is one of the workplace's most strong motivators. This idea was understood by the Westinghouse studies of the 1930s and concluded that workers are more motivated by personal recognition than financial benefit. An empowered culture should make subordinate contributions regularly and immediately recognized. Furthermore, leaders play a major role in this critical factor: while everyone wants praise for their major achievements, the real impact is when leaders compensate workers for their small contributions. Leaders actively seek to catch workers doing something wrong in some businesses and then reward them on the spot. Such systems ' impacts have dramatic effects on the quality of workers.

Employees Provided with Positive Feedback and Communication

Another key role for leaders in the empowered atmosphere is to effectively connect and provide positive feedback to employees. The leader promotes progress and motivation by inspiring and assisting the subordinate person to achieve their goals or goals. This is opposed to a director or boss who, if they fail to perform, directs and oversees employees. Similar to the two models, the emphasis on negative and positive attitudes is distinct.

Employees and leaders behaving with discipline

Confidence is not a haphazard fad of leadership, but a formal discipline within the company. This encourages workers to devote their efforts to their maximum capacity and thus enables a largely untapped asset to be used by the organization. Because it is a systematic approach, both managers and workers are directed to work within the parameters set by the organization's priorities, goals, expectations, and measurements. Barriers and restrictions are eliminated, but all workers continue to work for and towards the interests of the whole company. To maintain discipline and empower workers, bonuses and punishments are given.

Empowerment at Work

The word "empower" is strong and effective. These are often used, others say "overused." They are also misused. The most common misunderstanding of the idea of empowerment, similar to the theory of "motivation," is that one person can empower another. As I use the term, empowerment is an inner-to-outer process, most useful when accompanied by silence and inner guidance knowledge. Empowerment is not just another way of "doing" something, it is a state that fully supports you in living life.

Empowered individuals Empowered individuals are healthy, optimistic, aware, vital, compassionate, and prepared. Those motivated are not washed down, confused, hostile, divisive, or needed. Many motivated people, of course, have days or moments of uncertainty or anger or doubt, but the prevailing expression is one of self and others ' confidence and strength and consideration. Empowerment can also be contextual, meaning that in one situation you can think and be empowered, but not in another.

Many people like to be in the company of those who are genuinely inspired, but obviously not all, because the energy in and around them is infectious and soothing. Empowered people are keen on laughing and enjoying the moment in a way that helps others find their own strength. As powerful people shine their light, others can find their own light more easily. Often imitates the conduct of empowered people, but empowerment is not just a set of actions and behaviour. For true empowerment, acts associated with inner wisdom and strength are essential. Enlightened consciousness is not the other way around, but the root of motivated behavior. Since empowered people are powered from within, they bring with them their energy.

As I said in a positive way above, let me be clear here what empowered people do not do: empowered people do not get their energy from other people. Empowered people do not strike or overwhelm or trample on the rights of others, make offensive comments, ignore others, use negative language, control meetings, or disrupt others. Empowered citizens are not giving their power to others-nor are they allowing others to take their power (which is actually a variation on "giving power back."

You have to expel outdated beliefs, heavy vibrations, repressed fears and resentments in order to be motivated. To be motivated, you must substitute those who are empowering for disempowering values. You need to be mindful of the direction of your attention, your emotions, and your feelings to be motivated. Find your own expectations and beliefs and feelings and the desires and beliefs and feelings of others to be motivated. Start where you are right now without feeling wrong or thinking you need to be "fixed" to be empowered. Empowered organizations Empowered organizations are made up of empowered people, although it is not necessarily true that a community of empowered people automatically make an empowered organization. Truly motivated companies have broken out of the old paradigm of unfair rivalry and small and scarce values. Most people, including me, like to see the empowered organization evolving and shifting into a "new paradigm." Empowered organizations have transformed themselves into the new paradigm so that they can show such characteristics as: clear and honest interaction, teamwork within and between work units (usually called teams), shared responsibility in all aspects.

Individuals in empowered organisations are likely to talk about the "joy" of working and feeling "love" for their teammates, even though such words may not be articulated or are evidence of encouragement in such terms.

Many people agree with the desirability of principles such as "open communications," "collaboration," and "customer-driven" objectives. Set expectations, however, also stop the acts that bring these principles to fruition from being embodied. In many organizations, mistrust still prevails, particularly those facing downsizing attempts that have been or are being conducted using brutal methods. Belief that a company is in business to earn money alone keeps businesses locked in stagnant trends.

Where an individual or organization is right now, it is important to respect. It just doesn't work to push a new model on an existing one. From the inside out, lasting change occurs. The old paradigm's organizational structure is linear and upright: top-down and bottom-up. In many conventional companies, breaking the chain of command is an offense, increasing this linear approach.

The linear and vertical motion tends to change to horizontal or circular as organisations decrease or otherwise alter their structure. The old method of seeing what the one at the top of the company needs changes to look inside in order to determine with the aid of instinct what serves the highest good. Some of the popular names for the new organizations associated with this horizontal-circular-inward structure are: "group," "cluster," "learning community," "circles," and "networks." I consider the "flattening" of organizations to be fascinating and forward-looking with my window of thinking at energy fields and interacting with energetic concepts. When it occurs, flattening (eliminating management layers and other realignments) may not sound very good, but the end results may be extremely positive. The new forms and habits of working and working together to do business evolve out of the chaos. The theory of chaos that has arisen over the past few years will help you understand this process of finding and constructing structures of all kinds.

Who is empowered?

You are motivated, not because of your friendship with others, because of who you are.

Empowerment comes from within, not from outside.

This energy is used for the benefit of all, driven by high purpose.

Competition leads you to believe that there are limited resources.

You know that imagination is limitless when you transform inside, leading to unlimited resources.

You play with a limited power conviction.

With unlimited power you are empowered.

Support someone else be inspired today.

Such an act can help you to find your own strength.

Steps to Empowerment

It can take many forms to empower people. In most organisations, most steps can be taken to begin empowering people without financial risk to the company.

There are motivating habits that can bring enormous amounts of energy and leverage from the largest profit organization to the smallest non-profit corporation.

Here are ten behaviors motivated by conduct to empower people.

1–Create a chance of trust. Confidence comes from the performance. Results emerge from a combination of incentives and acts. It is possible to establish the climate at all rates. Identifying the more trustworthy people, the stronger. The same is true of the untrustworthy.

2–Include commitment acknowledgement. Most managers do not rationalize this by claiming that the individual was just doing their job. Question: Since when a service is shipped, error-free, on time and to a consumer spec only "do their job?" And give up a weekend and a family picnic to get a schedule back? Or do double shifts work to fix a consumer error in a time-sensitive assembly? Perhaps heading to a job site with a 4-hour notice in a foreign country to deal with an upset client? Recognition is rewarding at every point for a job well done.

3–Through the rules. It's essential to structure, no doubt about it. But the laws are either not explicit, ignored or obsolete in most organizations. Procedures offer direction-and flexibility-and motivate individuals by offering a route to achievement. Why was this wheel continuously wasting time and opportunity to reinvent what-do-do we-do?

4–Create concrete strategies and include individuals who can contribute to the system. This can be complicated-just write down what to do is so much simpler. Yet commitment empowers people and adds so much to setting goals. And the targets will be more hostile in most situations than if they had just been written down by the manager. Empowered people are working more and more intelligently.

5–Acknowledge the performance. This is unique, but just as important as remembering commitment. When a goal is met, encourage the people involved by acknowledging the accomplishment of the target to go out and do more.

6–Create action boundaries that permit some threat. Threat-averse organizations, for good reason, do not like to hear the talk of "any level of risk." Everyone wants a rogue bond trader, an unethical prosecutor, a deceptive accountant, an overly aggressive dealer to be bagged and tagged. Yet setting expectations based on the worst possible scenario restricts individual initiative that can not withstand autonomy, let alone flourish.

7 –Using chance as an achievement bonus. It should still be done, but it's surprising how many companies and individuals do not see resources as a bonus, but as a risk. In every company, pessimists have their position-they provide important control points and

healthy skepticism. But the future belongs to the optimists-the prospects seekers.

8–Ask what people think. And then listen to your replies. When I wrote about the most dreaded terms in industry-" What do you think? "Such words sound like giving up their God's right to lead to the command and control managers. The reality is that these words allow them to lead. And their people are motivated. It's time for a change if the managers can't see that.

9–Don't let your bums wear you. How often have sharp edges of people been identified as "just having to round off a little?" But a blunt instrument results in too much rounding off. Inside their "universe" of people, every director or leader has had multiple experiences that have the potential to reduce their own effectiveness-making them a blunt weapon. Bad bosses, bad or non-existent role models and mentors, deceptive and dual colleagues, bad circumstances–they all have the ability to wear down a person. That is why it is so critical and inspiring to have positive and optimistic values and aspirations. They stop the unavoidable unpleasant experiences from becoming the engine of behaviour.

10–Find out variations and promote them. No confrontation, there's no reading. Empowerment comes from different perspectives-and appreciation for those viewpoints. It is often tempting to shrug off the dissenting opinion or argument or suggestion, but allowing the opportunity to opinions to be included results in greater autonomy-and more successful decision-making.

Test your own actions against these 10 measures. So act to take the measures that make sense for the situation of the people around you and your situation. The result of these acts will be enhanced empowerment.

CONCLUSION

The word ' self-empowerment' does not appear in the thesauruses of my desktop, nor in my own Essential English-or Oxford dictionaries at home, whether spelled with or without a hyphen.

There are all kinds of others, but not self-empowerment, self-whatever.

Therefore, in describing what self-empowerment means to me, I am left to my own devices. A self-empowered person, to me, is someone who has found peace of mind inside him or herself in realizing that each person has his or her reality inside him or herself. Realizing that there are many, not just one, truths can result in each individual's understanding of the right to follow their facts.

Then the question arises whether this information will lead to chaos-if everyone does just what they want?

The response is NO-not when people have inner self-empowerment awareness. Misuse of thinking and profiting for monetary gain will be part and parcel of any modality that no truly self-empowered individual will or is morally capable of making cheap compensation.

Self-empowerment in this context is something that comes from the mind of an individual. It's not about money, social status, or how much it can be shown. You can't see self-empowerment; you can't buy it and it's not on sale at the closest retail outlet. I say, can you imagine that? For a few weeks or months, it would become a bling product, deliberately advertised by

Hollywood's finest sales reps as a "have-to-have" and then discarded for the next best thing-completely hollow and meaningless.

Furthermore, self-empowerment is not inborn self-assurance, whereas self-assurance is not a vital ingredient in self-esteem. Self-empowerment is what one acquires by life experience acquired knowledge.

Self-empowerment is a personal knowledge that you are the highest authority of your own. It's all about who you are and what you are. It's about you as a human being, not about any other body. You can't touch self-empowerment, but you can hear it. Others may sense your self-empowered condition as well, but they can't touch it physically. You may be able to affect it emotionally, but that will depend on your state of mind's strength and conviction.

Others will "see" a force in you— a hidden force that does not need external support— and they may be afraid of you and turn to blackmail tactics in an attempt to undermine your self-worth; especially when they are seen to be "superior" to you in some way in your social or work life.

I became quite disillusioned with some people in the last couple of weeks and ignored those who helped me in different situations and thoughts. I was trapped in the proverbial belief that "enough is enough" and forgot about my true self.

After this afternoon sipping some ginger tea on the grass, it came to me that if you walk a spiritual/holistic path, you're likely to arrive at a time when you realize that it's harder than you first imagined; and then to top it all –the realization that you can't actually turn back the clock after allowing Spirit to "in," so to speak.

Sometimes you just have to sit back and look at the trees to realize that life is a beautiful cycle if you just allow life to run through universal intelligence.

Overcoming yourself (with other words, freeing yourself from other people's expectations) and putting forth your true self is scary, but empowering thought. The saying of "moving on" with your life; "pulling yourself and getting over yourself" is when superiority is found in not being any single identity-and that's just the. Not so? And a master knows he/she wants to do that on their own.

In this awareness and behavior of no-identity, one finds order-even in the face of a world that assaults with a branding device everything.

Only with you is your true identity. Living this experience in your life is living life from the viewpoint of the soul.

Simply put-everything is in the mindset.

Taking the above-mentioned advice; where does one than lead? Saints and sages of yesteryear like Gandhi and more recent authors like Deepak Chopra have all talked and talked about the essence of love because the essence of love is the extension of your own identity as the lover. Wonderful! Very good! But what does that mean in fact?

The one who ends up living a balanced life is the one who has control inside-the one who knows that they are an equal partner with God-symbolically taking the hand of what we can't see in our 3D linearity and not placing it on an unattainable pedestal and turning it into an unattainable goal. That's the one with dominance, and that's the one with which everybody ultimately wants to be.

The desire for a spiritual path that strengthens a person is the product of combining the human heart with the love of God.

A person who is bound to the life-drama sway-thus living to live-is the one who puts stock and hope in being let down by others, including the one who is closest to them. Most times your heart will be broken and you will break the hearts of others. You are going to blame-including blaming new loves for the transgressions of past lovers.

Roots are for the unhealthy. Your "rootedness" must be in you, not outer systems or external philosophies. A belief in the "rootedness" of the outside (when the views of others form our identities) can contribute to your aspirations and beliefs being let go-replacing your imagination with dogma. You will feel strongly inclined to defend this assumptive identity once you have established a particular definition-this is a furtive ground for the bland ego. The egoic mind will devise all possible strategies to convince you that you are not worthy or self-sufficient.

Whether you feel you are bad, it will also be assumed by other people.

Living from your soul's viewpoint is understanding and respecting others as they are! Not just saying it, just knowing it and always meaning it. It's a lifestyle, a lifestyle, and part of your life perspective. Every waking moment will be with you and it will pass to every phase of consciousness and unconsciousness. And there you'll realize where others were in life and you'll embrace who they've become. You will also embrace who you have become without a doubt and encourage others to grow and welcome them to grow.

Lightning Source UK Ltd.
Milton Keynes UK
UKHW020710241120
374002UK00010B/575